my faith so far

Published by Jossey-Bass
A Wiley Imprint
989 Market Street, San Francisco, CA 94103-1741   www.josseybass.com

No part of this publication may be reproduced, stored in a retrieval system, or transmitted in
any form or by any means, electronic, mechanical, photocopying, recording, scanning, or
otherwise, except as permitted under Section 107 or 108 of the 1976 United States Copyright
Act, without either the prior written permission of the Publisher, or authorization through
payment of the appropriate per-copy fee to the Copyright Clearance Center, Inc., 222
Rosewood Drive, Danvers, MA 01923, 978-750-8400, fax 978-646-8600, or on the web at
www.copyright.com. Requests to the Publisher for permission should be addressed to the
Permissions Department, John Wiley & Sons, Inc., 111 River Street, Hoboken, NJ 07030,
201-748-6011, fax 201-748-6008, e-mail: permcoordinator@wiley.com.

Jossey-Bass books and products are available through most bookstores. To contact Jossey-Bass
directly call our Customer Care Department within the U.S. at 800-956-7739, outside the
U.S. at 317-572-3986, or fax 317-572-4002.

Jossey-Bass also publishes its books in a variety of electronic formats. Some content that
appears in print may not be available in electronic books.

All Scripture quotations, unless otherwise indicated, are taken from the HOLY BIBLE, NEW
INTERNATIONAL VERSION®. NIV®. Copyright © 1973, 1978, 1984 by International
Bible Society. Used by permission of Zondervan. All rights reserved.

The song on page 39, "I believe in Jesus," is by Marc Nelson © 1987 MERCY/VINEYARD
PUBLISHING ADMIN. IN NORTH AMERICA BY MUSIC SERVICES o/b/o VINEYARD
MUSIC GLOBAL INC. (ASCAP). All rights reserved. Used by permission.

Library of Congress Cataloging-in-Publication Data

Dodd, Patton.
My faith so far: a story of conversion and confusion / Patton Dodd.
p. cm.
ISBN 0–7879–6859–5 (alk. paper)
1. Dodd, Patton. 2. Evangelicalism—United States. 3. Christian biography—United States. I.
Title.
BR1643.D63A3 2005
289.9'4'092—dc22
2004014532

Printed in the United States of America
FIRST EDITION
HB Printing   10 9 8 7 6 5 4 3 2 1

my faith so far

A Story of Conversion
and Confusion

Patton Dodd

JOSSEY-BASS
A Wiley Imprint
www.josseybass.com

Contents

Prologue: Throat Clearing—The Who and
the What and the Why   ix

1. Conversion, As Best As I Remember It   1

2. God's Music   17

3. The Spiritual Exercises   31

4. Megachurch, Megafaith   47

5. Go Ye Therefore   65

6. The Categorical Imperative(s)   85

7. The God Who Is Where?   105

8. Charismania   121

9. The Fall(out) of the Holy Spirit   139

10. Arrested Development   155

Epilogue: The Never-Ending Story   171

Acknowledgments   175

The Author   177

To Ted, Kyle, and Michael—
three who have made a difference in my faith so far

Prologue
Throat Clearing—The Who and the What and the Why

This is the question that begs: Why do you believe in God?

It is a good question for anyone who does. When my friend Amy asked me early in 1995, I had a clear answer. A few months later, I did not. Amy asked me out of nowhere—we were driving around talking about nothing, about anything. We had just seen *The Brady Bunch Movie* and eaten ice cream. She halted our good time with sudden seriousness:

"Why do you believe in God?"

She expected me to stall. She knew I had been a Christian for about one year, and I was still in a wondrous state of religious conversion, a euphoric pleasure that had as yet gone uncritiqued. But I surprised her.

"I know exactly why I believe," I said, sitting up straight in the shotgun seat and preparing for some dashboard pounding. I really *did* know. I had been waiting for someone to ask me. I had a litany of reasons. I had a testimony, and I testified.

There were two problems with my answer.

1. It was based entirely on me. I said what I believed God had done for me, and although it is true, to paraphrase Frederick Buechner, that theology begins with autobiography, people who ask "Why do you believe in God?" are not necessarily looking for testimony. Testimony is good as far as it goes, but does it go far enough? One is never quite sure. It explains one's interpretation of one's own life, but perhaps the questioner is looking for more than subjective interpretation. "Why do you believe in God?" usually means "Why should *anyone* believe in God?" or "Does everyone need to believe

in God?" The question is not really about you, but God. Alas, testimony is still the best way for me to answer the question today. I can say other, more apologetically correct things, but not with complete confidence.

2. I was not prepared for the question to reproduce itself. Once you start asking *why*, it doesn't leave you alone. *Why* is never satisfied. Why this God? Why this faith? Do you have any evidence? Should you? Do you believe in Christianity only because you were raised in a Christian family? Were you raised in a Christian family only by virtue of having been born in a Christianized country? What would you believe if you were a visitor from outer space who arrived on Earth, surveyed your religious options with objective clarity—reading history and science and the Qur'an and the Bible and the Bhagavad Gita and *Dianetics*—and arrived at a cold hard logical conclusion?

We will never know.

The question is a luxury and a drain, and the available answers can be too idiosyncratic, too complex, or too dull. The state of Why Do You Believe in God can seem very poor indeed. Fortunately for me, and you, I will not be trying to answer that question here. I will merely be showing what happens when one does.

Believe, that is.

• • •

There is no one to blame but me. I hereby absolve all other parties from guilt in this matter.

If in what follows at times I appear to blame others, it is because at one time I did. Sometimes I still do, but I try to avoid it. I could have been wiser. I could have avoided some of these struggles. I own my own confusion; I will not put it upon anyone else. I would like to blame Oral Roberts and his eponymous university, which I attended for one year. I would like to blame Oral's son, Richard. I would like to blame Contemporary Christian Music and, well, the entire evangelical Christian industrial complex. It would be easy to do so, but too easy. Dishonest, even. I have a love-hate relationship with all those people and things. I loved them all before I hated them all, and I never quite gave in to the hate. I love them even now, though in a proportionally different way than before.

This is the story of trying to find that way.

· · ·

This is the story of a speck of faith. A mustard seed, you might say, but you would be wrong, because you would be overstating it.

This is a contemporary religious story, a tale of the times: a suburban kid flirts with slight danger in high school and college, then gets his head on straight by finding religion, then realizes his head is more crooked than before, then has one crisis of faith after another provoked by everything from boredom to banality to (John) Barth. He keeps thinking that he will figure some things out by the time he is twenty-seven or twenty-eight. But now he is twenty-seven or twenty-eight, and although he has figured some things out, he has also learned that much of what is substantial in life is what gets decided early on. Can you escape where you come from? Can you shed your skin? Once an evangelical, always an evangelical. If not in terms of belief or practice, then at least in terms of mental residue. They say you can never go home again, but you can never really leave home, either.

This is the story of a religious zealot who begins to question both the religion and the zealousness. He is upset. He points fingers. The bad guys are dcTalk and other Christian music artists, Jacques Derrida and other contemporary philosophers, televangelists, Christian higher education, the concept of a Quiet Time and other formulations for knowing God, Christian acquaintances who cannot be stomached. And William Wordsworth, Saul Bellow, and Quentin Tarantino. So, mostly it is a battle with evangelical brethren, and then some secular antagonists thrown in for good measure.

But that is not a good measure, no, not at all. It assumes the worst of all parties involved (except the zealot). So the zealot takes a step back and throws himself into the bad-guy mix, finding that he fits quite well there. He will see that some Christians entertain the same ideas as he—listen to the same songs, watch the same movies, read the same books—without devolving into despair. He will see that some Christians are smart, even-keeled, and fair. They reject the parts of their belief systems that don't hold up and embrace the parts that do, rather than trying to hang onto the whole package like a toddler with a toy. They critique redemptively rather than cynically. There may be problems with Christianity as he has experienced it—big problems that must be addressed—but he can also see how much of the badness can be traced back to him, because his response to the bad was as bad as the bad. And that's not good.

This is a retelling of a very old story: conversion and confusion, acceptance and rejection, spiritual highs and psychological lows. It is a story of coming to grips, of developing the ol' love-hate. It is about accepting articles of faith with the ease of ordering a sandwich, then having digestive difficulties. And negotiating a relationship with your culture after realizing that you are not at home in it, that in fact you loathe it and want to reject it, but also that (gasp!) the culture you give is the culture you get.

• • •

Midway on life's journey—or, rather, really quite early—I came upon myself in a dark evangelical wood. How hard it is to tell what it was like, this wood that was at once familiar and strange. The thought of it brings back all my old fears; but if I would show the good that came of it, I must speak of things other than the good.

This is not to say that evangelicalism is Dante's hell; oh no, nothing quite so drastic as that. Evangelicalism gets a bad rap for some good reasons, but for not-good reasons, too. It does have levels that can seem to descend ever deeper, and there are moments when one feels that one is in a *bolgia* of unspeakable horrors, where hearing a particular sermon or listening to a particular Christian pop song or reading a particular book is like witnessing Ugolino gnawing on the head of Ruggieri: ugly and awful and God-how-can-this-be? But there are equal-and-opposite moments, too. And one does not always begin in Inferno, head down to Purgatorio, and then climb the mountain to Paradiso. Sometimes one begins halfway up the mountain, or thinks one does, and then realizes that one is even further along the journey than previously thought—or, alas, not very far along at all. One keeps thinking that one's Virgil is a very poor guide indeed, because what he calls heaven seems like hell, and the path he says leads to hell turns out to be no more than a resting area.

The very first lesson is that lessons are forthcoming, because one is on a journey, and the distance between the *selva obscura* to the "love that moves the sun and the other stars" is sometimes very great, and other times only a step.

• • •

This story begins when I am eighteen and ends when I am twenty, and even charting the territory of those two small years has proven to be complicated cartography. Walking through the past, even your own past, is like being a pioneer: just as treacherous, daring, and indefinite as treading toward the future—even more so, because the events all require reconstruction and are laden with the terrible truth that you have recreated them in your own image. You are the dust that has settled over your own history. You remove the layers of yourself to investigate yourself, sometimes using a steam shovel, and at other times a feather.

Harder still is answering the question behind the question, the one that has beleaguered me these past several years: not "Who was I then?" but "What made me into the kind of person that I was then?" Not "What is the story of my life?" but "What were the historical and social forces that shaped the culture that shaped me?" I might be able to tell you how the A + B of my life equals the C that I became, but what about A in the first place? What made me a historical possibility?

When I became a Christian, I did not merely convert to a set of religious and philosophical ideas. I converted to a culture. And not just a Christian culture, but a type of Christianity that was different from lots of other types of Christianity that were potentially available to me. I did not become a follower of Christ *qua* follower of Christ. Without knowing what I was getting myself into, I became a charismatic. A Pentecostal. A social conservative. An evangelical, Bible-believing, chest-pounding Christian. More precisely, I became certain shades of all those things, as each of those terms contains variations that are not immediately apparent.

Right after I converted, when people asked me how it was that I became a charismatic Christian, I would preempt the conversation by claiming evidence of charismatic renewal throughout the history of the Christian church. Look at the church fathers, I'd say. Check out the mystics, and even the post-Reformation preachers like Jonathan Edwards. You will see plenty of evidence for healing and prophecy and *glossolalia*. Prayers for physical healing and demonic deliverance are nothing new, I would say glibly—Jesus did it, remember? I would claim that my experience of Christianity is of a piece with the Christian experience . . . you know, as *God* intended it. To be a charismatic Christian, I would suggest, is to be a super-enlightened Christian, a Christian from time out of mind.

That is what I used to say.

If there are shards of truth to that claim, the story that follows makes clear that I am the product of more recent historical forces. Pentecostals and charismatics (the two terms, as will become clear, have been conflated in my experience) can trace their American roots to several sources within the last two centuries. One place to begin is with Phoebe Palmer, a Methodist who felt she experienced a dynamic, sanctifying encounter with the Holy Spirit in 1837, and then set out to tell everyone about it. Her following became massive, and her teaching on holiness reverberates to the present day in many Christian circles. Palmer's following was just one of several pockets of revival in the late nineteenth century that highlighted doctrines such as postconversion baptism in the Holy Spirit, and physical healing, and dispensational premillennialism. The different revivals emphasized different kinds of ecstatic experiences and doctrines, but all were coalescing toward a Christian movement that would broadly be thought of as Pentecostal.

Most charismatic Christians today might have even shorter memories, looking to 1906 and a deserted church on Azusa Street in Los Angeles to find the roots of their praxis. In that year and the years following, Southern California opened its arms to receive two kinds of low-class refugees who would go largely unnoticed for a while before taking the nation by storm: those seeking fortune (and a year-round shooting climate) in the burgeoning (but not yet respectable) motion picture industry, and those seeking salvation (and a postsalvation second act of grace) in the racially mixed (and even less respectable) holiness revival. Hollywood arose from its urban, indigent roots to become the world's most wealthy and powerful media force. At a slower but similarly undaunted rate, the kind of Pentecostal Christianity practiced in William J. Seymour's Apostolic Faith Gospel Mission on Azusa Street and other revival sites across America followed much the same trajectory. Indeed, the revivals featured their own versions of superstar directors and actors, their own D. W. Griffiths and Gloria Swansons—such as Alexander Dowie, a controversial and nationally recognized turn-of-the-century revivalist, and Aimee Semple McPherson, a gorgeous evangelist who founded the Foursquare Gospel Church. Like cinema, Pentecostal Christianity was often embraced initially by the middle-to-low-and-no-class masses and shunned by the social sophisticates, but it eventually transcended class distinctions and morphed into a sedimentary—if shifting—social constant.

The Azusa Street revival and others like it carried on for several years, institutionalizing themselves in various Pentecostal denominations, including the Assemblies of God. This kind of ecstatic Christianity was, if not unprecedented, more widespread and permanent than any such revival that had preceded it. By the 1920s and 1930s, several Pentecostal denominations were in place. These groups managed to spread throughout the nation, gaining an ever-higher degree of social respectability, even being permitted to join the National Association of Evangelicals in 1943.

But in some sense, the character of many of today's charismatic converts can appropriately be said to have a still-shorter history.

Shortly after World War II, a new generation of superstar Pentecostal leaders arose, causing the movement to flourish as never before. This time, rather than denominations, the revival's high-profile front men formed independent ministries. Underneath big tents across middle America, men such as Oral Roberts made converts under the awe of the Spirit's power. Healing revivals filled auditorium-sized tents from the Southwest to New England. Pentecostal Christianity spread like a benevolent virus, infecting even mainline denominations and post–Second Vatican Council Roman Catholic communities. The revival was felt in virtually every part of America. It continued to thrive among the poor and uneducated, but Roberts and others helped carry it to the upper classes through the Full Gospel Business Men's Fellowship International, and first-rate universities such as Notre Dame experienced their own spontaneous student-led revivals.

By the 1970s, Pentecostal Christianity was all the rage. As many as five million Americans were caught up in the movement. High-rated television shows were produced, including a star-studded prime-time Oral Roberts show. Conventions were held in sports arenas. Universities were founded. Political figures were seen milling about charismatic gatherings. Thousands of books were published putting forth charismatic Christian doctrine and lifestyle. New styles of Christian music arose, along with new spins on prayer, worship, and fellowship. These new spins developed social weight of their own, suddenly looking like wisdom of old, like capital C Christianity, like God's Way.

Pentecostalism, then, is a new old thing. It has old precedents and new characteristics. Old ideas, new packages. To me, it was both new-new and connected to something old-old. It felt just right.

• • •

What is always surprising about historical developments is how quickly they become intractable. Within one generation, Oral Roberts is gaining influence; for the next generation his particular spin has the authority of doctrinal and epistemological backbone. By the time I happened upon Pentecostal Christianity in the early 1990s, it was a civilization, identifiable and widespread. To those within it, it was like an ethnicity, but without the bloodlines. To those within, it was The Way the World Worked.

It has been an act of near sacrilege to acknowledge the recent history of my faith culture. Admitting that there is a set of historical circumstances leading up to my experience of Christianity was tantamount to admitting that my experience was somehow arbitrary—a historical chance. An anomaly. Not necessary. Not inevitable, but conditioned upon variable people and places and things. This was not good. My faith was supposed to be essential, out of time, a perfect revelation of God I received from God Himself, unmediated by personalities, technologies, and popular Christian music.

When you embrace your surrounding culture wholeheartedly, you run the risk of bracketing off its history, its particularity. You run the risk of believing that it is just How Humans Are or How Humans Should Be. Then, when the curtains are pulled back, you think, oh crap, it didn't have to be this way. This is arbitrary. I am arbitrary. Everything I believe is arbitrary.

You do not understand this. You shake your head. "Of course there is a history to your history!" you exclaim.

But you are reasonable, and I was not.

When my faith fell apart, it was because I saw that my knowledge was social, and I became scared that it was *only* social. I saw that there was a cultural personality to my belief system, just like all the other belief systems in all the other cultures. If my faith is a result of social forces, I thought, then it is not the result of pure spiritual forces. I was not the kind of Christian I was because that kind of Christianity was essential. I was the kind of Christian I was because I lived in Colorado Springs in the early 1990s, which coincided— incidentally, absurdly, not inevitably—with the arrival of a major evangelical charismatic presence in the town, a presence that caught me in the right place at the right time.

If knowledge is social, I thought, then belief is social. Religion is social. God is social. There was, I could see, a kind of pluralism within the family of God—if that family could even be said to exist under such circumstances.

All my experience as a Christian had to be rethought in light of this terrible realization.

● ● ●

The idea of Christianity is rooted in the belief that there is a rationality to the way of the world, a reason for who we are and what we do. The Christian faith claims to have extraordinary explanatory force, touching all. Everything must be interpreted in light of this belief; it is when odd or unsettling things happen that the belief is really tested, and sometimes it must adjust to experience. Lesslie Newbigin reminded me of this just recently as I read one of his books, and I realized that my early Christian faith was limited precisely because it had no capacity to adjust. Christianity as I understood it held little ability to explain anything. Its reserve of nuance and flexibility was used up very quickly. There were lots of events and ideas that my faith did not touch. I let my faith be too small, too confined to variable traits, and it was never the all-encompassing, ever-insightful, world-explaining hermeneutic that I believed it to be.

This, then, is the story of that hermeneutic, and why it had to fall apart, and why I'm glad it did.

Evidently I grew out of this state of infancy and reached boyhood. Or should I say that boyhood grew in me, replacing infancy? For infancy did not go away. Where could it have gone to?

—St. Augustine, The Confessions

my faith so far

Conversion, As Best
As I Remember It

The date is September 7, 1993. My six-disc CD player contains these albums:

1. *Core*, by Stone Temple Pilots
2. *Crimson and Blue*, by Phil Keaggy
3. *Nevermind*, by Nirvana
4. *The World As Best As I Remember It, Volume 2*, by Rich Mullins
5. (no disc)
6. (no disc)

These are the only four CDs I own. The CD player is my first, and having saved for it all summer enough money remains to buy only the four discs. Yesterday, I went to Target and bought STP and Nirvana along with the CD player, and then drove over to a Christian bookstore, the Lord's Vineyard, to buy the Phil Keaggy and Rich Mullins albums. I barely know who they are, but I have determined to listen to Christian music, and Amy Grant and dcTalk are out of the question.

After months of deliberation, I have decided to become a Christian. I have been a Christian all my life in a "check your religious preference" sort of way, but now I am *becoming* a Christian, which is entirely different. *Being* has to do with status and voting habits and family Christmas traditions. *Becoming* has to do with daily practice—what to think, what to say, what to read, where to put one's foot down and why. To my thinking on September 7,

1993, becoming a Christian means many things, but mainly these: that I will stop doing drugs, that I will start reading the Bible, and that I will start listening to Christian music. These three things may have very little to do with Christianity, but on September 7, 1993, this is what makes sense.

The Rich Mullins album sounds like middle-of-the-dial Easy Listening Hits, but I dig Phil Keaggy a lot. I listen to *Crimson and Blue* every morning while I get ready for class. It sounds like the early Beatles in all the right ways, and track seven is a cover of a tune—a Van Morrison tune I have never heard ("When Will I Ever Learn to Live in God?"), but Van Morrison all the same. Keaggy has a guitar-god voice, which means he is better when he's playing than when he's singing, but the mix is somehow brilliant. And when he just plays, he *wails*. I love this album. My old tape collection is a catalogue of classic rock, and Keaggy baptizes that sound. I can rock out and be spiritual at the same time. For several mornings in a row after I buy the album, I get out of the shower, lie on my bed, listen to Keaggy, and drip dry.

I tell very few people about this. Slowly, quietly, by myself, I am becoming a Christian, and I am doing it on my own terms. I have chosen to spend a year attending a local university in my hometown, Colorado Springs, so that I can focus on changing my ways, and on campus I play it cool with my old friends. They invite me to get high after class; I make excuses. They invite me to parties, but I know I cannot go without . . . partying, so I make excuses. It is not long before we go our separate ways. Other friends have left town for other universities, so I have a lot of spare time on my hands. I study. I go to church. I play "Street Fighter" on Sega. I lie on my bed and listen to Christian music. I read the Bible in big, thirsty gulps. I think I am becoming someone completely different, and I am. In a matter of weeks, a tumultuous shift has occurred in my thinking. I have unzipped a layer of skin, stepped out of it, and donned a new one. I quit everything at once: no more pot, no more drinking, no more swearing, no more lying, no more sex.

No more anything but Bible and prayer and Jesus.

The church I attend is a charismatic megachurch on the north end of town, just off the interstate at the edge of the city limits. I do not know what *charismatic* or *megachurch* means, but that is what people tell me this church is. In years to come both those terms will take on grating complexities, but for now I like them. I like saying them. "I go to a charismatic megachurch. Charismatic. Megachurch." The words are bulky and sweet in my mouth, like a Jolly Rancher. *Charismatic* means that this church, and therefore this faith, is unlike the boring Southern Baptist Christianity of my youth. *Megachurch* means huge and exciting and powerful and nontraditional. It feels new and squeaky clean, and I am hoping it will help make my soul feel the same.

The exterior of the church looks like a Wal-Mart with half a paint job: a blue-and-light-blue concrete box surrounded by acres of parking. Situated as it is several miles east of the foothills of the Front Range of the Colorado Rockies, at the beginning of the plains that stretch eastward for eternal miles to Kansas and beyond, the blue church is backed by nothing but a blue sky, rendering it at once ominous and invisible. There is no landscaping to speak of, no steeple pointing toward heaven, no bulging masonry, no graveyard to signal that this is a church of the old marrying-and-burying kind. It looks, in fact, less like a church than any building in town. But this isn't a turnoff. This is an important advantage—it permits me to walk in feeling nonreligious. I am not looking for religion. I am looking for God. Indeed, I hardly even notice the building's aesthetic misfortune. It is what happens inside that counts.

The main meeting room is massive and square—high ceilings, flat floor, plain walls. It is a still sea of blue chairs, no waves, no undertow. The room has no frills at all save the three jumbo video screens located above the stage so the folks in the back can see the pastor. This is exactly what I need. I am a little lonely without my old friends, but I want to live a clean life and I feel I need to be alone right now to do so. I want to be in church, and this is the church I want to be in. It is so crowded that I can slip in and out unnoticed. It is so casual that I can wear sandals and shorts. The pastor keeps saying that God loves us no matter what we've done. I love that idea, and I want to learn how to love Him back.

This time last year—even this time last *month*—I spent Sunday mornings showering off the smell of pot before I saw my parents at breakfast. Now I spend them dancing before God. Really, actually dancing. At this charismatic megachurch, people dance hard. They jump and spin and flail their arms about. They shout from fully expanded lungs: "Hallelujah!" "Thank you, Jesus!" "You reign! You reign! You reign!" These folks are unabashedly excited about Jesus, and I think that is cool. I want to be excited about Him too.

The first twenty minutes of each worship service are packed with fast-paced songs of praise. The songs are not much for lyrics, but they get straight to the point:

> *Let Your spirit rise up in me!*
> *Let Your spirit rise up in me!*
> *You set my feet a'dancing*
> *And my heart rejoicing*
> *And my mouth singing out Your praise!*

Or:

> *Alive, alive, alive forevermore!*
> *My Jesus is alive!*
> *Alive forevermore!*
> *Alive, alive, alive forevermore!*
> *My Jesus is alive!*

For us, they say all they need to say. We want to sing and dance before God, and the music does not give us any other choice. The band rocks—a pianist and two guitarists and a bassist and a trumpeter and a drummer and a choir and a lead singer who appears at all times to be totally lost in the moment. I think one would have to have a hard heart indeed not to leave one's seat and dance down the aisle. I do not want to have a hard heart, so even when I do not feel like it, I force myself to dance. I jump and spin. I develop little jigs. Sometimes I just pound the floor with my feet as hard as I can. On Mondays, my ankles ache all day.

When the twenty minutes of pulse-raising praise music are over, there are twenty more minutes of slow, soulful worship. At the charismatic megachurch, we don't merely genuflect. We crumple to our knees. We sing "More love, more power; more of You in my life" and "Precious Jesus, You are worthy of all praise." We sing from our hearts; no, lower; we sing from the bottom of our bellies. I weep during these songs as I think about my sin and how Jesus loves me anyway. In one forty-minute span, I go from awe to joy to sorrow to humility to deep, deep gratefulness. The gratefulness is what I like best.

Praise and worship, as the musical portion of the worship service is called, is an emotional roller coaster. But it is one that I get on every Sunday morning, so I know every twist and turn and loop-di-loop. It doesn't leave me exhausted. It leaves me simultaneously fulfilled and longing for more.

As the months turn into years, the services won't change much, but I will. As I do, the recent memory of the services will, by degrees, confuse, comfort, or convict me. There will be times when I long for those early days of easy faith. There will be times when I pine for a completely different past. There will be times when I believe that who I was just after conversion is nothing like who I was before or who I became later.

But for now, my head is clear and my heart is full. I leave church Sunday mornings feeling as if my soul has been scrubbed clean. I am simmering with faith. When I get into my car to drive home, I turn on Christian music and sing it at the top of my lungs. I want to sing all the time.

I am becoming a Christian, and I absolutely love it.

• • •

Every conversion story has a back-story. Turn the calendar back to one year earlier. On September 7, 1992, I have only a dual tape deck, and it holds Led Zeppelin's *Houses of the Holy* and the Black Crowe's *Shake Your Moneymaker*. It is my senior year of high school.

I have a mullet. (I was a little slow coming into the nineties.) My sister, Kaysie, has recently moved back into the house with my parents and me. She had been away at college and then living in the mountains, and when she returned she was a very devoted Christian—the fiery, excitedly spiritual type whose faith oozes from her pores. Kaysie has always acted Christianly, but something is notably different now. She is not overbearing, just devout and sincere. She is happy. She seems to have a fresh perspective on life, like someone coming home from a motivational conference.

My sister had always exerted a pleasant authority over my life. Five years older meant five years wiser. She defended me from neighborhood bullies when I was seven, let me tag along on dates with her boyfriends when I was eleven, and prodded me through the awkwardness of junior high with tender joviality. At every stage of childhood and adolescence, I have wanted to become who she was. Until now. When she moves back into the house, she cramps my style. I can't come home during lunch to get high because she might be there. I can't sneak out my window after midnight because she is in the adjacent living room watching a movie. I have to be more vigilant than ever. She will see my carefully cultivated Good Boy Routine for the load of crap that it is. For a high school senior, this is a terrible irony: Kaysie—short, thin, too amiable to resent—casts a deep shadow of responsibility over my life.

Starting that fall, Kaysie invites me to come to church—the charismatic megachurch—with her every week. I gently refuse. As contagiously happy as Kaysie is, it is still church, and I know it will either be infinitely boring or make me feel guilty, or both. The refusals don't agitate Kaysie, and they don't bend her resolve. She is not quite pushy, but she is not passive either. She takes the suggestive "Patton, you should come to church with me" approach rather than the inquisitive "Patton, I was wondering if you'd want to come to church with me sometime" approach. My answer is always the same: "Yeah, you're right. I really want to. I think I'll come next week."

This clever defense works several times. For a couple months, it satisfies Kaysie and prevents us from getting into a conversation about why I do not go to church and what my life outside the house is like. But in time the look on Kaysie's face becomes more and more sour with every refusal, and wanting to make my sister happy one Sunday I go. Then I begin to agree to go more often than not. Hungover, stoned, whatever, I crawl out of bed on Sunday mornings just a couple hours after stumbling through the door and go sing songs about God and listen to a preacher.

I don't really enjoy it, but I understand it, more or less. I know all about God and Jesus and the Holy Spirit and Eternal Salvation and Hell. I was raised Southern Baptist and was part of a church youth group until I was fourteen. My parents quit forcing the church issue in high school, and I was more than happy to let it drop.

So in 1992, as of my senior year, I have not attended anywhere regularly in years and think about God about as often as I think about chicken soup. But with Kaysie back in the house, God is in the air again. She makes Him unavoidable. The more involved she becomes at church—the more she has people from the church over to our house, the more her Christian boyfriends try to befriend me—the more I remember that I was raised to be a good Christian boy, and now I most certainly am not.

To my horror, our house soon becomes the weekend gathering place for Kaysie and her church friends. I have already perfected the art of coming in quietly on Saturday nights so as to spare my parents the sight of their drunken son stumbling to his room. Now I have to learn the art of coming in and smoothly hanging out with a bunch of Christians lounging in our family room watching *Forrest Gump*. I have to cross the family room to get to my bedroom, making it too suspicious not to say hello but too dangerous to plop on the couch next to my sister reeking of alcohol. I choose an inconspicuous spot on the floor off to the side, ingratiate myself into their presence ("Hey guys. Oh, *Forrest Gump*. Cool.") and count the minutes until I feel I have sat still smiling at the TV long enough to convince everyone that I am not intoxicated, that the beer/pot/cigarette smell emanating from my clothes and hair is stench by association, that I am the perpetual designated driver for all my misguided friends, and that Kaysie sure is proud to have a brother who is hip enough to be out with the cool kids but well-raised enough to walk the straight and narrow. I sit and smile in the general direction of the television until I believe that everyone believes this.

Kaysie never bothers me about these awkward evenings. I know she has to know, but we seem to have a mutual silent agreement that going to church on Sundays is my penance. I go, and she leaves the previous night's embarrassment alone. She mentions from time to time that she would love to talk to me about "what's going on in your life," but she never prods.

Nothing unusual happens before January of my senior year. New Year's Eve is lame as usual; my friends Carlos and Matt and I perform our yearly ritual of driving from party to party on December 31/January 1 and complaining about them all. School is still out for winter break, and things are rumbling along quite nicely. I have good friends. I have a girlfriend. It is the last semester of high school. I am happy.

But for some reason—not for any specific circumstantial reason that I can remember, but there must be a reason—on the first Sunday of January 1993, I decide that I need to become a Christian. A Real Christian. Nothing has gone wrong that needs fixing, and I am not desperate to alter my lifestyle. It is merely a logical decision that I make one weekend on the basis of the previous few months' experience of church with Kaysie and stoned conversations with Matt and Carlos: I believe there is a God. I believe He wants me to be a good person. I believe that if I am not a good person, I will go to hell. Hmm. I had better make sure I am a Christian. Plus—and this is at least half of the matter—I am tired of hiding things from Mom and Dad and Kaysie, and I have to hide everything—and I know it will be a whole lot easier to tell them about all the things I have been doing if we are all under the emotional spell of a fresh repentance.

I go to the megachurch with Kaysie that Sunday, and as the service begins I play out the scenario in my head: I will wait until the end of the sermon, when the pastor asks if people want to accept Jesus into their hearts. I will raise my hand, go to the altar, pray a prayer, and officially commit my life to God. I will stop sinning and be a good person. All my friends will be shocked, but hopefully they will be jealous of my sense of contentment and my satisfaction with my eternal destination and my ability to love everyone and still be a cool guy. I will be a funny, exciting Christian that people will want to be around, and surely before the end of the school year all my friends will be Christians too and we will walk down the hallways holding our Bibles and we will be coming to this church together and we will love life ever so much.

The more I think about it, the more excited I get. This morning is going to be the beginning of something great. This morning I will give my life to Jesus, and my world will be remade.

Even before the pastor has begun his sermon, I am looking forward to getting home and surprising my parents with the good news. I take in every word of the sermon, and when he invites all the non-Christians to come to the altar to become Christians, I am the first one out of my seat. I walk to the front of the church. The pastor prays a prayer with me and the fifteen or so other people at the altar. We confess our sins and our need for God and say that we accept His love for us. We are ushered into a room in the back of the church where I pray some more with another pastor, a muscular, mustachioed, longhaired man with a toothy smile lodged deep into his tanned face. He sits too close to me and holds my hands so tight I think they will crumble, but his presence is warm and I don't mind, much. We finish, I sign a little card, check the appropriate box ("What do you want to do this morning?" the card asks. The options: "Accept Salvation." "Renew my commitment to Jesus Christ." "Receive information about becoming a Christian." "Receive information about becoming a church member." Not quite sure where I stand, I check the first two.), shake his hand, and walk out to begin my life anew.

Voilà.

On the ride home, I tell my sister about a couple of dirty things I have done. She is aghast but pleased that I have decided to stop doing those things. It feels good to speak the unspeakable. I can 'fess up, get things off my chest, and not suffer any consequences. I decide here and now that I need to tell my parents everything too. *Everything.* I will come clean, get a fresh start, and spend the rest of my senior year of high school living right and telling all my friends about how great it is to live for Jesus.

When we arrive home, I walk in from the garage with my sister, peer downstairs into our family room, and call out to my parents.

"Mom, Dad, we need to have a talk."

My parents shuffle up the stairs. I point to the kitchen table, directing him to one end, her to the other. I sit in the middle. My sister disappears into her room. I feel bold and new. I feel re-created. I want my parents to see that the son sitting with them at the kitchen table is the New, Improved Patton. I will show the sins of the past to contrast them with the sanctification of the present. They will be ecstatic and we will all have a wonderful afternoon eating popcorn and watching the Denver Broncos.

Thirty-minute-old confirmed Christian that I am, I figure the best tactic is to blurt out all my sins at once.

"Well, Mom and Dad, today at church I gave my life to Christ. I believe in Him completely now, and I'm going to live a different life. And I think the first thing I need to do differently is be honest with you."

My dad stares at me through his glasses. My mom watches the stove. Then they look at each other.

"Mom, do you remember a few months ago when you asked me if I ever did drugs?"

"Mm, hmm . . ."

"I'm sorry, but I lied. I want you both to know the truth."

Blank stares.

"I want you to know the truth about everything."

Blank stares.

My dad finds his tongue. "Which drugs do you do, son?" He is missing the point entirely, but I figured this was coming. I grimace with seriousness.

"The usual suspects, I suppose. Pot. Acid. Crystal meth. Nothing too dangerous."

More blank stares.

"And some cocaine—but not snorted. Just sprinkled it on my pot. Same with the crystal."

More blank stares.

"And the scar on my lip—it actually *didn't* come from a skateboarding accident. I was wasted and passed out onto the pavement."

No response.

"I guess I've been living a different life away from home. I haven't been in trouble at school or with the police or anything. I've been smart about it. But it's like . . . I just do these things. Like sometimes I get high with my boss at work before I come home at night. Stuff like that."

Nothing.

And so it goes for some time. Blunt revelations followed by blank stares. My parents—Mississippi-bred, down-to-earth, sincere religious folk—are dragged through the mud of their teenage son's recent past in the service of an exciting new conversion. I know I am telling them tame tales in comparison to what many of my friends are doing; I have always walked my own version of the straight and narrow. But for my parents, this is serious stuff. They are stunned, shocked, irritated, but what can they do? God has forgiven me, and they have to as well! Sure, I was rolling joints in my room as recently as yesterday, but today I am a changed man. The prodigal son has come home.

("Oh, and Dad, that time last year when the car was out of alignment really bad and the hubs were all trashed? Remember how the axle almost snapped apart while you were driving? That was my fault too. Carlos and I had bounced it off a curb when we were racing. I'm sorry I lied about that.")

Of course, some of this is stuff they suspected, but I have been a darn good liar and always lucky enough not to get in trouble. Most of my friends have been busted at one time or another for underage drinking, drugs, stealing cars, etc., but I managed to fly under the radar of the cops, the school, and my parents. Now, the thin veneer is being pulled back, and it is liberating. Exhilarating. The more I talk about my former darkness, the more I feel I am coming into the light. I feel like I have gone down to the river in a train of sorry souls, gotten baptized, and come up singing, "Glory, hallelujah!" I expect that at any minute my parents will join me in ebullient celebration.

Instead, my mom begins to weep softly. This is not something I expected. I explain to her—again—that all I am doing is telling them the things I *used* to do. I am not like that anymore! "I'm really excited about church now, Mom. I love it. I don't want to do those things anymore. I want to become a strong Christian and help all my friends become Christians."

"I understand that, Patton. But who do you do drugs with?"

"Mom, that's not the point. I can't tell you that."

"Is it Matt?"

"Mom, I can't say. It doesn't matter. The point is—"

"But we've got to know what you're doing when you go out of the house now. Did you and Carlos get drunk at his house last weekend?"

This is no good. All I want is to be a good Christian, and they can't see it. Humbly and sincerely, I tell them I understand their frustration, and I promise that they have nothing to worry about. I am a new man, and I am excited about learning how to live for Jesus. The conversation ends with my dad telling me that if I get a girl pregnant, he will kick me out of the house. My mom climbs the stairs to her room and quietly shuts the door. I sigh. I shake my head knowingly. I silently forgive them both for their lack of faith. I tell God I know I have dishonored them in the past, so I understand their frustration. I pray that they will forgive me. They will come around in time, I am sure. Amen.

The next week at school, I walk on air. I even take my religious conviction for a public test drive, telling a couple of people that I have become a Christian and won't be partying anymore. It feels great, and they are oddly supportive and congratulatory, as if it is something they have always wanted to do too. My girlfriend says she wants to come to church with me. Everything is proceeding as planned.

Then, on Thursday, my friend Dan says John has a bag of good weed at his house. They are skipping final period to go smoke. Do I want to come?

I hesitate, shift from one foot to the other, and offer to drive.

It is an arduous smoke. Time is supposed to feel gradual after you smoke, but that afternoon things shift into slo-mo well before I ever put flame to weed. It takes us ages to walk through the school hallways, get into my car, and creep through the parking lot. My car is filled with five or six guys, their weight pulling us down into the street. Arriving at John's, we can't get into the front door. I climb the fence into the backyard and break in. Once we're all inside, John can't find his pipe, and we root the trash bins for aluminum soda cans. Finally John digs out a nasty old homemade water bong from his closet, and we smoke. But getting high is terrible. I am moody the entire time. I drive over to Carlos's house, let myself into his basement room, and sleep it off. I wake up hungry and guilty.

The next night, I attend the megachurch's youth group service. I find the mustachioed guy who prayed with me the previous Sunday morning and tell him what I have done. He smiles as I explain everything. When I finish my story, he says that I need to be baptized in the Holy Spirit. I am not sure what that means, but he says it will help me resist things like pot. I say OK. He takes me to the side of the chapel and stands just inches in front of me, looking me straight in the eyes and placing his strong, veined hands on my shoulders. His face is kind and warm. He looks as if he is going to reveal the secrets of life to me.

"Now," he says, prepping me, "I'm going to lay hands on you and pray for you to receive the Holy Spirit. The sign of receiving the Holy Spirit is speaking in tongues, so just open up your heart and let it happen."

I follow him vaguely. "Lay hands" is plain enough, though it seems to contain some hidden meaning. I know the Holy Spirit is God, but I don't understand how I can receive Him if I don't already have Him. "Speaking in tongues" bangs around in the back rooms of my memory but finds little purchase; it too rings a faint bell in the Church Language category, but one that won't resonate fully until later.

I don't find any of this off-putting, though; I take my unfamiliarity with his terminology as an indication of the sinful condition of my mind.

The deacon closes his eyes and tells God that we are asking for the Holy Spirit to come upon me. A few moments pass, then he starts speaking softly but firmly in a gurgled language: "Shoka nana, shoka nana, keel nonamba! Shoka nana, shoka nana, keel nonamba!"

I listen and wait. I tell God I want to receive the Holy Spirit. I wait some more. Nothing is happening. I figure that if it is working, my lips will start moving themselves and the gurgled language will begin pouring out. I tell God I am open to the Holy Spirit.

Finally, I whisper, "Hey, um, nothing is happening to me."

"Yes, it is happening! Just let it come forth from you. God is baptizing you in His Spirit. Just pray like I'm praying."

Slowly, bumpily, I force the sounds out of my mouth. "Hooh nananano, sheekorima." Ooh, it sounds horrible. The deacon does it so naturally, and I sound like one of the Sand People on Tatooine. But as I speak, the deacon starts praising God, so I figure I am doing something right. "Hooh nananana, sheekorima. Washinogama freekozena."

"Alright!" he says. "Praise God! You're being baptized in the Holy Spirit!"

We keep praying for several minutes, and I continue feeling as though my gurgled language is awkward and his is cool and he is just being nice about it. But the deacon explains that it is OK if it does not come naturally at first. Every believer in Christ has a spiritual prayer language, and it is up to each believer to exercise it. He says that if I pray in tongues as often as I can, I will be a more powerful, stronger Christian.

I want to be a more powerful, stronger Christian, don't I?

I do, and what he says is convincing. I came to the church youth group to find out how to say no when my friends asked me to get high, and this was the immediate answer, so I figure it is the right one. It is probably what the Bible says to do. I imagine that this guy has had lots of people like me come up to him with this problem over the years, and that he has always told them about the Holy Spirit, and that it always works, and that's why he smiled knowingly when I told him about my problem. And he is very nice about the whole thing even though I know I did not do it right.

Within a few weeks, I am absolutely convinced that I did not do it right, because I am smoking more pot than ever before, and any inclination toward church or God or righteousness or pleasing Kaysie and my parents is gone. It is the last semester of my senior year, and more than anything else, I just want to have a good time.

2

God's Music

Evangelical Christians can be an anxious lot when it comes to popular music. In the minds of young evangelicals, as in the minds of young nonevangelicals, music signifies overly much about social standing. We—especially those of us who grew up with two social circles (church youth group, and public school friends)—are fantastically worried about our status as cultural outsiders. We want to be in. We want to be relevant. But we know we are out. We fear we are irrelevant. We feel we have been given a terrible choice: either Michael Landon and *Highway to Heaven* or Angus Young and *Highway to Hell*. For us, Coolness and Goodness are completely polarized. All of the high school and college social terror that exists in the mind of every teenager is compounded for evangelicals. Do we have the right taste? Are our t-shirts hip? Is our hair long enough? Yes, we believe in Jesus, but please don't group us with Pat and Jerry! We're nothing like them. We go to rock concerts! We've seen Radiohead twice! We drink socially, if moderately. We read novels. We watch all the independent films. We're trying, really.

Music is the biggest indicator of our dilemma. Our parents want us to listen to Steven Curtis Chapman and dcTalk. (If you do not know who they are, it just means you are inside the mainstream of American culture, or else you are outside in a different way. Chapman is a clean-cut singer-songwriter. dcTalk is, or was, a three-guy band whose music is either rap or grunge or rap-metal, depending on the nation's musical mood. Both are, or were, rock stars within Evangelicaldom.) Our parents want us to listen to anything approved by a Christian label. We want badly to listen to anything approved by

MTV. We may agree to attend the occasional Jars of Clay (also Christian rock stars) concert, but we will not breathe a word of it at school. This is a constant battle, and even church kids who are convinced, as I was, that they *should* listen to what their parents want them to listen to, often do not. And, like all teenagers seduced by the industry of cool, we mostly ignore the innocuous stuff and go straight for the foulest, the stuff that is sure to offend our parents and pastors. When I was fourteen, I knew that DJ Jazzy Jeff and the Fresh Prince had some cultural cachet and were nearly as harmless as dcTalk. But I listened to N.W.A., who were infinitely cooler.

Christian music is an industry and a culture, known as Contemporary Christian Music, or CCM. It is an alternate universe with its own techno, grunge, and pop-acoustic acts; for every popular rock genre, there is a CCM corollary. It began, by most anyone's estimation, in the 1960s and '70s with Jesus musicians such as Larry Norman and Phil Keaggy taking popular forms of rock 'n' roll and using them to communicate clearly evangelical messages. Christian groups had descried the effect of rock music on the youth of America, but the Jesus musicians addressed the problem from within. Don't bring the kids to the church, they said. Take the church to the kids in the only language they understand. Norman put the Christian music dilemma front and center in one of his most popular songs, "Why Should the Devil Have All the Good Music?" Why indeed, went the consumer industrial response, and by the late 1970s Christian rock had its own production and distribution lines and was focused on getting itself into the hands of kids like me.

We were the first generation to have an opportunity to be raised entirely on Christian pop.

As a young kid in a Southern Baptist household, I assumed that the problem with rock music was one of style. Rock was evil because rock could only be evil. The guitar solos, the drums, the long hair—it had all the makings of a demonic scheme. But from its very beginnings, Christian musicians took the position that music is morally neutral. No matter what the form, they said, music is little more than a tool, a carrier of messages. CCM postulates that it makes no difference if one is strumming a harp and humming softly with eyes closed or finger-hammering a guitar and screaming into a microphone. It doesn't matter, as long as the message is that Jesus Christ saves sinners. Step into a Christian music shop today and you can find a Christian band forged in the image of Korn—tattooed and pierced and angry, only their rage is directed at Satan—or a Christian diva who is a fully clothed version of Britney Spears.

And they are plenty good at what they do. The Christian industry of cool is adept at whitewashing the popular sounds and fashions that inhabit the mainstream industry of cool. Popular Christian musicians are often just as skillful and professionally produced as the stars of Top Forty radio, and if you put a Christian Country artist next to a mainstream Country artist you might not be able to tell the difference unless you pay attention to the content of the songs. Both will sing about broken hearts, but one will suggest that hearts can be mended by Jesus.

Growing up evangelical means that turning on the radio involves a moral decision. Baptist churches like the one I grew up in encouraged us to take a moral high ground in our music selections. Sunday School and youth group made the matter black and white: I could listen to Christian music and please God, or listen to secular music and please Satan. That's what I was told as a twelve-year-old in church youth group, and the things you hear as a twelve-year-old in church youth group stick with you. The music sounds essentially the same on both sides, parents and preachers would say, so why not listen to music that glorifies God? The logic was hard to refute, partly because to admit there *was* a difference was to admit that cool mattered overly much. And it should go without saying that the strict moral dichotomy between secular and Christian music rang true every time I listened to the radio or watched MTV. When I was a sixth grader grappling with these complexities in 1986, Steven Curtis Chapman was singing about how much God loves everyone and about trying to be a good husband. Motley Crüe was singing about strip clubs. God's music was cheesy, but it was clean. The devil's music was evil, but it was cool. I was always much more interested in Cool than Clean, but I was never able to quite give myself over. Even in my most rebellious days, I kept a couple of Christian albums around for good measure. The things you are told as a twelve-year-old in church youth group stick with you.

For years, Christian music was the only kind available in my house. I didn't even know there were any options other than the Beach Boys, who my parents felt were harmless enough (if only they knew), and movie soundtracks like *Annie* and *Robin Hood* and *The Rescuers*, all of which we had on vinyl and all of which I memorized. When I was in the third grade, I was given my first Christian rock audio tape, *Not of This World* by Petra—a long-haired, leather-clad glam band, equal parts Toto and Air Supply. Petra was like a gateway drug, ensuring that I would forever be hooked on rock music. Electric guitar. Drums. Synthesizer. A lead singer with a girl-ish, screeching voice. The album cover had a guitar-shaped space-ship flying through outer space. I knew the music would take me to the outer reaches before I even turned it on. I had a hot pink shirt and black sunglasses and I'd play Petra on my oversized 1984 boom box and sing to the crowd in my room. I took Petra to school and showed it to all my friends. I had the vaguest notion that it was a Christian album, but mostly I just knew it was rock music. My friends didn't seem to know the difference either. It wasn't as though Petra sang about Jesus much, anyway—they sang about the dead rising and angels warring and feeling like an alien. (Perhaps their outsider status was not lost on Petra. The title track goes: "We are strangers; we are aliens. We are not of this world." The song is about how Christians are not supposed to feel at home in the world because our home is in heaven, but it might also be about how Petra could never get play on Top Forty radio.) Regardless, they were momentarily hip to my fourth grader friends and me.

Extremely momentarily. My buddy Chris had a slumber party for his tenth birthday; we rocked out to my Petra tape for a while and then watched the world premier of Michael Jackson's "Thriller" video on MTV. Entranced by Michael and the Creatures of the

Night, everyone forgot Petra immediately. I slid Petra into my bag, a little saddened that my parents had bought it for me while Chris's parents had bought him the *Thriller* album.

When I was in the fifth grade, Kaysie began to listen to secular radio stations loudly in the house. It was her own mild rebellion, and Mom and Dad let it go. She still sang in the church youth group choir, after all. Every morning I would wake up to the sounds of Chicago, Whitney Houston, and Prince. Petra and other CCM favorites—WhiteHeart, Mylon LeFevre and Broken Heart, Michael W. Smith—gathered dust. How could they compete with Jermaine Stewart's "We Don't Have to Take Our Clothes Off"? With WhiteHeart, I could multiply forgiveness seventy-times-seven. But with Jermaine, I could dance-and-party-all-night-and-drink-some-cherry-wine-uh-huh.

There was nothing catchier. Within a few weeks of listening to secular radio, I knew that it was not the music that was better, but the whole package. The effect. The *affect*. The ethos. The deejays. Everything was carefree and modish and it offered immediate entry into What Everybody Else Is Doing. The allure of this music on my mind and body and soul was something that Petra simply could not duplicate. Phil Collins and Culture Club and the Bangles: I knew I should resist them, but I could not. These folks were not just cool—they were the arbiters of cool. They Built This City on Rock and Roll.

Still, I could not escape the feeling that listening to secular music was doing something dirty. I loved that feeling, but I knew I shouldn't. In the sixth grade, I lived in the basement of our rental home, far away from Mom and Dad and the world upstairs. Every night I would go into my room, shut the door, and listen to the *Top Nine at Nine on 98.9 MAGIC-FM*. For weeks, I could count on the fact that George Michael's "I Want Your Sex" would be played during the countdown. It was the most titillating thing I had ever heard (well, it might have been the *first* titillating thing I ever heard). I would dance and dance and sing and sing, making sure to stay near enough to the radio that I could change the station the moment a parent walked in. "Sex is natural, sex is fun. Sex is best when it's one on one." Oh, they would not want their twelve-year-old singing those words. And, yes, well, I should not be singing them. True, true. It was wrong. It was dirty. It was so much fun to listen to.

So from Petra to George Michael to Eazy-E I went, though in high school my moral code was more complex. Drugs and alcohol could be consumed without guilt, but I felt a terrible twinge whenever I listened to Black Sabbath. Led Zeppelin was fine as long as I didn't believe the rumors about what happened when you played the album backwards, but Metallica was evil. (Until the *Black Album.*) Of course, I listened to everything, whether it was evil or not, but I had to carefully monitor my guilt in order to enjoy it all. For a while, I felt that actually attending concerts was not something I should do, so I let tickets for Alice in Chains opening for Van Halen pass me by, though I had both bands' songs memorized.

Later, when Kaysie was back home and God was back in the air and I had confessed my sins and gurgled in tongues but was still wondering whether I should make the leap into faith full and complete, it was perhaps inevitable that Christian music would be my entry point back into Christianity. Based on my upbringing and all that I had ever been taught about Things Secular and Things Christian, I knew that listening to Christian radio was a sign that I was trying to improve my life. It was like supporting a starving child. It made me feel that I was doing something good.

• • •

And in the summer of 1993, in the midst of all the pot and LSD and beer and girls and lies piled upon lies, in the midst of wondering about whether my conversion in January had meant anything at all, there was Christian music, acting as an annoying, convenient, and ideologically reliable rudder, directing me to where I (partially) wanted to go. I was not quite ready to give up my wicked ways or read the Bible, and I was certainly not willing to talk to the Holy Spirit Guy again, but I wanted to keep the question of conversion open to discussion, and Christian music was a much safer dialogue partner than Kaysie. It didn't require any immediate response. It just gave me an opportunity to think about God.

On days after parties when I had done something especially awful, I would drive around town and listen to a Christian radio station. The songs that played on that station were about love and forgiveness, and they opened up a space for me to consider what it would be like to live a supermoral life, a life dedicated to God. The deejay's syrupy sweet voice made me cringe, but she always hoped that I would have a "blessed" day, and I could hear her straining for authenticity. She meant it, or she wanted to mean it. The music was bad—horrible, actually, inexcusably lame—but I felt drawn to it nonetheless. I learned that Stephen Curtis Chapman and dcTalk were still around, as were Michael W. Smith and WhiteHeart, just as they had been seven years earlier. But their competition had changed from George Michael and Motley Crüe to Nirvana and Pearl Jam, so it was even more hopeless than before. Still, listening to Christian music was the Right Thing to Do, and it felt great to do something right.

It also felt great to be able to say, "Kaysie, have you heard of that group Pray for Rain? I like the first single off their new album." (Which was called "That Kind of Love." The song asked, "Where does that kind of love come from?" The answer: "They say that it runs in His blood.") Christian music did not merely answer a spiritual thirst; it answered a need for a homecoming. It was my childhood. It was my roots. It was pure and separate.

One night near the end of the summer I was driving around in Kaysie's Toyota Tercel, thinking and praying. I needed music to fit my mood, and I rooted around in her glove compartment looking for the right soundtrack. All she had was a bunch of popular Christian music and one secular album: *Chicago's Greatest Hits*. I looked at the Christian tapes one by one. *Lead Me On* by Amy Grant. *The Big Picture* by Michael W. Smith. *Freedom* by WhiteHeart. *The World As Best As I Remember It, Volume 2* by Rich Mullins. I was familiar enough with Grant and Smith and WhiteHeart to know I did not want to listen to them, so I popped the Mullins tape into the player. It was so awful to my ears that I could only leave the volume turned up for the first two songs. But I did not turn it completely off. I drove around and sorted through shelves of emotion; I thought about God and my life and my future and my family; I thought about being high and being sober. I thought about the Holy Spirit Guy. I tried to put it all together and see if I could find some organizing principle. Mostly, I thought about how I was beginning to hope that God still loved me. That idea held a kind of attraction that I had not recognized in a long time. And I knew that His love anticipated a response.

At some point, my ears tuned into the lyrics that were wafting from the speakers. All the clutter in my mind funneled into one stream and began to flow with the song. The music was so unlike the rock that I loved that I tuned it out entirely (my tastes, it turns out, were severely limited), but the simple lyrics simply overtook me. They made sense in a way that only songs can make sense. Song lyrics can be hackneyed and annoying and still come together in a way that reverberates, that reconciles and refocuses everything in view; it happened to me as I drove down the road and listened to Mullins sing about some woman telling him that love is found not in what is kept but in what is given up, and about how truth hits you hard in the middle of the night. It was a sentimental, weepy song, and I began to weep along with it. I pulled over to the curb and took the liner notes out of the tape casing. The song was "What Susan Said" and it was about two best friends growing up together, a lifetime of memories and meaning filtered through a friendship. In some way, it was about Matt and me, and later that year I would type up all the lyrics and send them to him in a letter, and I would make him a tape of this and other songs by Rich Mullins (who had by then won me over completely). Matt would call and say, "I hate that guy's music, but his lyrics are pretty good." I would know what he meant.

That night on the side of the road, I thought about our friendship, but mostly I thought about how I felt lost, and here it was in the middle of the night, and what Susan had said to Rich Mullins was being said to me right now: *Love is found in the things we've given up more than in the things that we have kept.* I cried silently at the profundity of it all, and deep inside myself I knew that I wanted to give up everything and keep nothing so that I could find as much love as possible.

• • •

Aside from, or in spite of, my impending conversion, the summer of 1993 was deliciously carefree. Matt and I both worked day jobs—I at AT&T, he at Kay-Bee Toys—and as soon as work was over we would meet at his apartment and settle the evening's business in as quick a manner as possible. Three questions: one, how do we get beer? Two, how do we get pot? Three, how do we get girls? Most nights, we would end up at a house party for a while, then return to his apartment to play Spades and smoke endless packs of cigarettes. It was, we kept reminding each other, the best summer of our lives. We had simple pleasures that were easily satisfied. There was no high school to return to, the first day of college seemed far off, neither of us had a steady girlfriend and therefore no one to tell us not to hang out with each other, and we had pretty much perfected the art of dodging our parents. We were on our own. All of our friends were in a good mood all the time. We had free time in abundance. Life was grand.

But even as I kept agreeing with Matt that our summer was going great, privately I knew it had been a mixed bag of mild teenage rebellion and thinking hard about whether or not I wanted, in the language of the megachurch, to "commit my life to Christ." Halfway through the summer I started going to services every Sunday night, privately. From 6:00 P.M. to 8:00 P.M. each Sunday I would sit in the very back, sing gospel songs and listen to the preacher talk about Jesus, and then hop in my car and speed to whatever party Matt was at. Within the hour I would be stoned, charismatic worship tunes still ringing in my ears.

Pot was helping my conversion process more than hurting it. After Sunday night services, all I wanted to do was think about

God, but I did not want to do it alone. I didn't want to talk with anyone; I just didn't want to be by myself. I could go to parties and be surrounded by people but smoke enough weed to carve out a mental space of my own. I would sit in the backyard with the rest of the stoners, smoke and smoke, and then go inside, find space on a couch, and act as if I was asleep. I could hear people around me: "That dude is so wasted." But I was not only wasted; I was lost in thought about Jesus.

One night at one of these parties, Matt poked me and said he wanted to go for a drive. We hopped in my car and pulled down the street. We got to the end of the block before either of us noticed the awful sound coming from my car speakers. It was Michael W. Smith's "A Place in This World."

"—the hell are you listening to?"

In truth, I had left the radio tuned to the Christian station on purpose. I knew when I arrived at the party that Matt and I would eventually be in my car together. I was already feeling a little evangelistic impulse, and I thought maybe Christian music would give me a way to talk to Matt about God. Plus, I wanted my friend to know what I was going through, and I wanted to know what he thought. Hopefully he would want to talk about Jesus too, and we could sit in my car and pray for salvation together and then return to the party.

Clearly, my hopes were too high.

"I don't know what it's called."

I knew exactly what it was called. I knew every lyric. The station had been playing "A Place in This World" every half hour for a month. For all my distaste for the song, I had heard it enough to memorize it.

"Well, it sucks," Matt said. Click. "A Place in This World" was immediately replaced by Alice in Chains's "Man in the Box." We were both happier.

But over time, I became bolder about my declining taste in popular music. I outed myself completely, in fact, confessing to Matt that I was seriously considering making a 100 percent commitment to God, and that's why I listened to Christian radio. "Not that it's wrong to listen to Zeppelin and stuff," I said, conflicted, "but I think I need to fill my mind with Christian things. At least some of the time." Matt was OK with that. He was even encouraging. He sure wasn't willing to listen to "that crap too, but not because I don't believe in God, man. I believe in God. I know there's a God. I was raised Catholic, you know."

As the summer wound down, bad Christian music became just about the only music I wanted to listen to, except when I was stoned. I knew that I was not just listening; I was learning how to be religious. I was learning how to have a relationship with God, just as the megachurch had advised. For better or worse—actually, for a bewildering mix of better *and* worse—Christian music was informing the way I believed in God. Life with Jesus was exciting and every day was an adventure (so said Steven Curtis Chapman). God's love was unexpected and unlike any other love (so said Pray for Rain). I was supposed to seek God in the morning and learn to walk in His ways (so said Rich Mullins). Popular Christian music was teaching me how to believe what I wanted to believe; it was inserting me into Christian culture; it was subtly shaping my impression of spiritual things. I would later reconsider my steady consumption of this particular expression of Christianity, but for now it was convincing me, in spite of its notable lack of cool, that I needed to become a follower of Christ once and for all.

At the beginning of August, Matt prepared to leave for college. I knew that as soon as he left I would make a commitment to Christianity. I wanted to wait until he was gone partly because I didn't want to ruin our fun while he was still in town. Matt appreciated this. We had talked about God enough at this point that he knew I was gearing up to become an honest-to-goodness Christian, and he had continued to be encouraging. He understood. He had thought a lot about God lately, too. He thought maybe when he got to college he'd look for a church. We both doubted that he really would, but still he was encouraging (and he would eventually prove us both wrong).

I drove Matt to his college, six hours away in Durango, Colorado. We got so stoned on the trip that we somehow ended up in New Mexico. It took us twelve hours to make the six-hour trip, and by the time we arrived I had to turn right around and drive back home.

A couple of weeks later, I decided that there was no use stalling any longer. I wanted to live for God, and I was sure the place to start was by getting rid of whatever pot I had on me.

The next day I went by my friend J.J.'s apartment so she and Brian and I could get high before class. We did, went to school, and then trudged through class. Afterwards, I nudged Brian as we walked out the door and asked him if he wanted to buy the rest of my bag. We walked to his car, he gave me ten bucks, and I gave him my pot and a couple of pipes.

"You're giving me these, too?" he asked, looking at the pipes.

"Yeah. I don't need them. I'm not going to smoke anymore."

He snorted. "You're not?"

"Seriously. I'm, uh, I don't know if I said anything to you before, but . . . I think I'm going to try to be a Christian."

" . . ."

"I know. But yeah. A Christian."

"And that means you can't smoke pot."

"I think so."

"Cool, man."

He shrugged. I shrugged. I got out of his car.

So, that was it. I had converted. This time I meant it. Stopping smoking was a symbolic gesture. It was, as far as I could tell, a religious sacrifice, giving up something I enjoyed because I felt it was standing in the way of my coming closer to committing my life to Christ.

I was an ascetic.

● ● ●

Two weeks later, I buy my CD player and the Christian CDs. I go to one more party, but I do not have the patience or gregariousness to party sober, and I do not know how to tell my friends I am a Christian, so I leave. Within a month, I am attending the charismatic megachurch on Sunday mornings, Sunday evenings, and Wednesday evenings. By late September, I am rising from bed an hour and a half earlier every morning to read the Bible and pray. I am attending prayer meetings. I am studying Christian devotionals. I am changing everything.

I am becoming a version of myself that will comfort and confound me for years to come.

3

The Spiritual Exercises

My alarm clock is set to go off at 7:30 A.M., but I am awake at 7:18. I smile as I realize that I will have twelve extra minutes of morning. I need as much time as possible, because I need to pray for the whole world.

The Christian discipline of having a Devotional (aka, Quiet Time) has given my days a ritual and a rhythm. I have never been an early riser, but now I am setting my alarm earlier and earlier each week as I find that I need more and more time to pray. My freshman composition class begins at 11:00 A.M., and initially I am rising by 9:00 so I can be showered and ready to pray by 9:30. This gives me a full hour before I need to be backing out of my driveway and heading to class. That hour is split: a half-hour for reading the Bible, a half-hour for prayer. But the split quickly becomes too little for both halves. My Quiet Times brim with activity.

To Bible reading I add Christian devotional material, books with titles like *The Quest for Character* and *Intimate Moments with the Savior* by people with names like Charles Swindoll and Ken Mire. These books are written specifically for people like me, people who have Quiet Times. A few pages of sermon-esque writing (pithy insights, poignant life applications) are followed by a Bible passage and suggestions for further Bible reading. To the Bible I go as directed, always reading more than assigned. More Bible is better Bible. There is no programmatic reading method for me at this point (that will come later), no Ignatian meditation exercises, no concerns about reading too little or too much (that too will come later). I can turn to the passages suggested by Swindoll, or I can just as easily flip the Bible open to a random passage. Either way I find transformative spiritual knowledge. Every page of the Bible fits in perfectly with the whole. I do not understand it all, but I believe that it is all understandable. I trust that in time I will get it all because it is all meant to be gotten.

I am not examining the text so much as I am letting the text examine me. I am not studying; I am being studied, seeing myself from within the pages of the Bible. It is as if I shrink to the size of a serif and walk about the crinkly pages, swinging from letter to letter, exploring the biblical wilderness to see what good I might find there.

When I read what Paul wrote about himself two thousand years ago, I believe that I am also reading about myself. His words fit perfectly into my context. I feel especially at home in the fourth chapter of 2 Corinthians, and I return to it frequently. "We have renounced secret and shameful ways," says Paul, and yes, this is what I have done. "This all-surpassing power is from God, and not from us." Right, and I need to remember to rest in that truth. I have not created these ideas; they are creating me. "We always carry around in our body the death of Jesus, so that the life of Jesus may also be revealed in our body." This gives me an entire posture, a way of appropriating the sadness of the world, of dealing with tragedy and failure, but also of grasping for light in the midst of darkness. The world is dead and alive at the same time, which explains the ambiguous middle in which we now live. And just as I am contemplating the struggles of each day, the chapter ends with a particularly Pauline punch: "Therefore we do not lose heart. Though outwardly we are wasting away, yet inwardly we are being renewed day by day. For our light and momentary troubles are achieving for us an eternal glory that far outweighs them all. So we fix our eyes not on what is seen, but on what is unseen. For what is seen is temporary, but what is unseen is eternal."

Yes, yes. Everything around me is wasting away. This explains why I snapped at Dad last night. It explains what I read in yesterday's paper about AIDS in Africa. It explains my friend John's struggles at school, and it explains my constant battles with lust, with fear, with selfishness. It explains why someone with so much new hope can still feel so scared, so weak—when my classmate made a snide remark about Christianity yesterday, why did I nod in feigned agreement? But Paul gives me a firm Christian optimism, a safe place from which to work on the world. It's all just a light and momentary struggle. If I can see it, it must be temporary. If I can't, it must be eternal, and therefore true.

Sometimes, especially when I flip the Bible open randomly, I do not land in places as easily applicable as 2 Corinthians 4. Sometimes I land in Psalm 137's "happy is he who repays you for what you have done to us—he who seizes your infants and dashes them against the rocks." On occasion I wander into Romans 9's "God has mercy on whom he wants to have mercy, and he hardens whom he wants to harden." Sometimes I read about Samson in Judges, and I cringe because it is precisely when the Spirit of the LORD comes on Samson that he obliterates his enemies. Or about King Saul, who is afflicted by the same Spirit of the LORD, which causes him to thirst for David's blood. Why would God's spirit do that? Is that not contrary to everything I believe about God? But for now, these biblical moments are only speed bumps, nothing more. I pause and wonder at them, but they do not drain the life of my Quiet Time. I know that there may be portions of the Bible that are temporarily beyond my grasp, but I will understand it all someday. It is God's perfect love letter to me, and I trust that it is consistent. It is the most important book in the world. I rest in its authority.

Some mornings, an hour passes in Bible reading, leaving no time for prayer. This is a problem, because I have not actually talked to God, I have only read about Him. I need to rise earlier. An hour of Bible and devotional books, followed by an hour of prayer. But I feel I need at least two types of prayer: Praise-and-Worship Prayer, and Intercessory Prayer. Praise and Worship is celebrating God, talking to Him about how good He is and how grateful I am for Him and His love. This is extremely easy for me. The praise pours out. I put on a CD of worship music and sing along, and I own the words of the songs. My parents have already left for work, so I can bellow, I can sing at the top of my lungs, and I do. I pace back and forth in the living room, my prayer volume rising. I wave my arms toward the ceiling and celebrate the greatness of God. I stand in the middle of the room, feet together, arms stretched out, head thrown back, and bask in His love.

Intercession is praying for the needs of others. To intercede for someone is to contend for them, to plead for them. Intercession is praying that all my friends will come to know Jesus. It is praying that my sick father will be healed. It is praying that Matt will be safe at college. It is praying that President Clinton will have wisdom as he makes executive decisions. It is praying that the people of China will be protected, that doors will be opened to the spread of the gospel there. It is praying for everyone and everything that I can think of. It is spreading spiritual help to people all over the world.

The charismatic megachurch stresses the importance of both these forms of prayer. The church explains that praise and worship will lead directly into intercession and intercession will lead back into praise and worship. They are right, and my prayers flow from one stream to another like a chain of tributaries. Thanking God for His goodness causes me to want everyone I know to experience that goodness. Praying for friends leads to praying for the whole city, for El Paso County and the State of Colorado and the United States of America. My prayers cover the nation, the world. They pour out of my mouth and gush through the air, rumbling up the foothills of Pikes Peak and leaping into the sky, splashing down into the plains and rushing across into the towns and boroughs and metropolises, seeping under people's windowsills and covering their entire homes like a film that won't come off. I imagine heroin-laden men in the ghettos of Harlem, thirteen-year-old girls about to lose their virginity in rural Georgia, bankers on Wall Street seeing their fortunes come crumbling, farmers in Iowa struggling through drought to bring about a harvest. I pray for spiritual revival in Los Angeles and Birmingham. I pray for the near and the far, and I feel that my prayers are changing the lives of people all over the world. They are prayers offered in faith. And faith, as I've learned at the charismatic megachurch, makes prayer effective, and prayer activates the work of the Holy Spirit to change the world.

The Holy Spirit is changing the world as I pray. How could it *not* take a full hour or two each morning?

• • •

The social world of the charismatic megachurch is a baptized version of the social world of high school. There are Preppies, Geeks, Stoners, Punks, Hipsters, Granolas. All are converted, or assumedly so, but few have left their fashions behind. On a given Sunday, you can look across the auditorium and see a cluster of denim jackets with motorcycle patches on the back, a constellation of carefully shaved or dyed heads, a gathering of vintage t-shirts, and a band of Gap jeans and pullovers in muted hues. The cliques are not nearly as stratified as in high school—there is mingling before and after the church service, and a general air of acceptance. If a Punk wants to hang with a Preppie she is welcomed, and if for the most part people tend to stick with their own, it's only because old grouping habits die hard.

By virtue of this being a suburban church, the Preppies are the most populated clique. Many are athletic and beautiful and, most important in this environment, they are all deeply spiritual. They can be seen visibly entranced in prayer a few minutes before each service begins, and several of them continue praying individually or in small groups for a good half hour after the service is over. These folks have it together. The social world at the megachurch is their entire social world. They throw barbecues. They play volleyball and basketball on the weekends. They rent movies. They meet over bagels and coffee. Most oddly, they get together to walk around the city and pray. They call it prayerwalking, and I have heard the pastor talk about it a few times. Prayerwalking is interceding for a certain area, like a school or a particular neighborhood, but doing it on location. Instead of sitting in your room and saying, "God, please protect the children of Carver Elementary School," you drive over to Carver and walk around and silently, discreetly pray, "God, please protect the children of Carver Elementary School." Prayer-walking is all the rage at the charismatic megachurch and, as I know from talking to my sister's friends, the Preppies do it all the time. I've not yet tried it, but to me it represents a level of spiritual insight that only the few attain, and I will want, eventually, to be among the few.

When I first begin attending church on a weekly basis, I see all these uncliquish cliques and know that I belong somewhere be-tween the Granolas and the Preppies (sad but true, as I wish I be-longed with the Hipsters). But for the first time in my life, I do not much want to be a part of a group. For me, for now, church is not for chit-chatting. Church is serious business. I come to each service with certain work to do, the spiritual work of growing in Christ, and I can do it best alone.

The megachurch holds services from 10:00 A.M. to noon on Sunday mornings, from 6:00 P.M. to 8:00 P.M. on Sunday evenings, and then again on Wednesdays from 7:00 P.M. to 9:00 P.M. I attend all three. My ex-girlfriend sometimes attends church with me, and she immediately ingratiates herself into megachurch society. I know that everyone goes to lunch after the morning services and to din-ner after the evening services, but I want no part in such gatherings. I do not want to meet and greet and shake new hands. I have re-cently lost most of my old friends, and I am cultivating, massaging, my loneliness. I need to be alone in church because church drains me of every ounce of emotional energy. The services unleash a tor-rent of feeling and knowledge. I am learning about the Most High God and What He Created and Why, about Our Purpose and Eter-nal Destiny. I plunge deeply into the song service, soak up every word of the sermon, and wade through the auditorium up to my waist in newfound truth. It is all I can do to get into my car and drive home.

So far, Christianity is driving me into a happy seclusion. During my weekdays this autumn, I find that I have discovered new plea-sures that require privacy—the aforementioned prayer, and study. Prayer keeps me in my bedroom longer each morning, and it sends me home right after class. I pray at regularly scheduled times each day, and I pray for long, spontaneous stretches throughout the day. I need to be alone because prayer might strike at any minute, and I want to be available.

Likewise, study encloses me in my room for long evenings, or pushes me into the damp corners of used bookstores for afternoons on end. I was a voracious reader as a child but have not read broadly or habitually in years, since before high school. Now, along with my faith in God, my desire to read and learn has been reawakened. I devour the Bible along with the books that are assigned to me in my university classes, especially my Introduction to Philosophy course. I had never heard of *The Phaedo* or René Descartes or Immanuel Kant and his Categorical Imperative, and it is all a whirlwind. Somehow much of it seems to be confirmed by whatever I'm reading in the Bible. I sit on my bed for hours, *The Critique of Pure Reason* opened next to Philippians. I am not so much checking one against the other as I am fascinated by both. The Bible has priority, but I am developing a love for pages in general. I read and reflect, and then lay back and pray about it all. I feel that my mind is engaging the many facets of God's big great world. I want to understand everything. I have no doubt that I can.

I am particularly turned on by Kant. The monographs I read explain that as the eighteenth-century German philosopher outlined his notions of morality over the course of several major works, he reacted against centuries of received ethical wisdom. How do we know what we should do? asked Kant. We know not because of the consequences of our actions or handed-down ideas of virtue, as was assumed, but because of a more fundamental, primary moral principle, which he called the Categorical Imperative. The CI is mainly this: "Act according to that maxim whereby you can at the same time will that it should be a universal law." In other words, the way to be moral—which, for me, means the way to be godly, the way to be a Christian—is to do things that I could suggest that everyone else in the world should also do. If I can say that everyone should do what I am about to do, then I can do it. This seems consistent with the new ideas I'm incorporating from the Bible and the charismatic megachurch—not least because if anything is a categorical imperative, believing in Jesus is. Faith is a moral action that the entire world needs to perform.

When I am not praying or reading or in school, I am working evening shifts at the mall or passively playing Sega. But the real rhythm to my week is set by the services at the charismatic megachurch. They help set the boundaries of my mental and emotional life. They chart the course from weekend to weekend. Each service is similar to the one before, but somehow better. The only difference between Sundays and Wednesday evenings is that the midweek service is strictly for young people; the guitars screech a bit more, the median age is younger, but the format is essentially the same.

Shortly before each service begins, I walk into church and navigate through the blue chairs to my regular seat near the front. The auditorium lights are up high; the place is as bright as a clinic. I sit and watch the band preparing their instruments, or I look at people mingling and gravitating toward their seats. At a few minutes after ten, people are still mingling, and the worship leader walks up the platform stairs and turns to his microphone as the band slowly, softly begins to play.

"Good morning, everybody," he says, low and soft and informal. "Let's get ready to worship Jesus."

We respond by standing in front of our chairs and singing along with a slow song of worship, following the lyrics on one of the three jumbo screens. This first song sets the mood, focusing our attention on God and the experience of worshipping Him. Then the tempo abruptly changes, and we sing three or four or five fast-paced praise songs. People move into the aisles to leap and shout and dance. Then the mood calms down again, and we sing twenty minutes more of slow songs, many of which are more inwardly focused than the praise songs—if we sing quickly about God's greatness ("Alive! Alive! Alive forevermore! My Jesus is alive!"), we sing slowly about ourselves, our sin, and our needs and trust in Him ("Refiner's fire, my heart's one desire is to be holy").

Often during the slow worship time we sing a song that sums up our creed, and I weep profusely. The sing-songy simplicitly somehow expresses the deepest hope of my heart:

> I believe in Jesus.
> I believe He is the Son of God.
> I believe He died and rose again.
> I believe He paid for us all.
> And I believe He is here now.
> Standing in our midst.
> Here with the power to heal now.
> And the grace to forgive.

These words make me shudder with their veracity. I sob loud, powerful, guttural sobs. I do not feel self-conscious about my strident weeping because everyone around me is crying, too. At this church, we rip our hearts out every Sunday morning and hold them high for all to see. It is emotionally exhausting, and it feels good in the way all workouts feel good. I leave the service knowing that God Himself has taken a spoon and scooped all the nastiness out of my chest and flung it into the stratosphere. I leave hollow and happy and return to each service with my chest cavity newly filled with gunk. I want to be Shop-Vac'd by God.

What is He removing, exactly? Doubt. Fear. Resentfulness. Lust. Every cigarette I smoked that week. Every lie I told—every exaggeration, every spin on the truth. He is removing anything that does not please His perfect will, and there is plenty to remove. Though I have spent years binge drinking and getting stoned and undressing girls with little guilt, now that I have found Jesus I realize just how guilty I have always been and will continue to be. It is a wonderful, blessed revelation. It feels good to know I have been wrong, and I know there is nothing I can do to be made right. God has to do it for me, and I believe He will. He is. He has.

Though I am aware of my sin, I am not riddled with guilt. I realize how much I am stained only by virtue of being closer to God's holiness. The praise and worship services push me right up next to Him, or else they bring Him down to me. The songs do for me what icons do for Eastern Orthodox Christians: they open windows to the divine. When we sing about God the auditorium seems to fill up with His love. We raise our hands and sway back and forth until worship takes us over completely. Every Christian feeling I can imagine occurs in the course of these songs: conviction for my sin; gratitude toward God; love for my family and friends; compassion for people in need; concern for the downtrodden; joy for life everlasting, or just for the sake of joy. The pastor has said that when we worship, God shows us what is on His heart. So what He cares about, I care about; what He feels, I feel.

As we worship, the church cliques melt into one buoyant formation of singing and dancing, kneeling and weeping. There are plenty of folks who stay in their seats and wear plainer expressions, of course, but several hundred of the three thousand-plus people have arms stretched into the air, bodies swaying to the sweet music, faces awash in all the varied expressions of religious devotion: Love. Desperation. Glee. Humility. Satisfaction.

I try to keep my eyes closed in order to concentrate on God while I sing, but inevitably they are pried open by the temptation of seeing people move their bodies in praise. At this charismatic megachurch, worship is a sight to behold. It is an austere dance of devotion. It is heavily serious and gaily playful at the same time, and it looks unlike anything I have ever seen.

Worship dancing is not beautiful or rhythmic, but it is a striking physicality. It calls attention to itself particularly upon one's first exposure to it, not because the dancer wants to be seen but because the dancer is a strange sight and one cannot help but gawk. The worship dancer will begin by hopping slightly, clapping or waving her arms in the air, or letting them bobble at her sides. This hopping may be all there is to the dance, but the more excited, daring, or uninhibited worshipper will follow the hopping with high bouncing—one gigantic leap after another, as if propelled by a trampoline, her arms pumping skyward and her voice shouting praises. After bouncing comes spinning, round and round, arms stretched perpendicular to the body at their furthest lengths. The worship spinner spins faster faster faster, turning the dance into play, being as carefree as possible before God. The spinning is dangerous and must be done carefully in a crowded church auditorium, but no one minds a momentary loss of control: if one stumbles or slams into a chair, it's OK—it's just part of the play. If there is space enough, spinning can be completely subsumed by running and leaping. Some dancers end their worship session by jogging slowly around the auditorium, smiles tugging at their cheeks.

This is worship dancing in general, but the first rules of worship dancing are improvisation and self-expression. Worship dance is ad lib dance; it is the unstoppable corporeal expression of a grateful heart toward God. Some dancers dance as at a rave. Some pace and flail their arms. Some wave banners and streamers and do a kind of ballet. Others run and leap, or kick their heels back, or hop on one leg. They do whatever needs to be done to celebrate their freedom in Christ, to proclaim how worthy He is of praise. "When the Spirit of the Lord moves in my heart," says one of our songs, "I will dance like David danced." People shout "Hallelujah" when that song begins to play, and then they perform it.

And some do not dance at all. Some of the people at the charismatic megachurch remain in their seats, bobbing gently or swaying to the music, stretching their arms toward heaven, or not; singing at the top of their voices, or quietly; closing their eyes and swaying, or standing stiff and trying to figure the whole scene out. I am, at one time or another, each of those people. But at this time, a few short weeks into my full-fledged conversion in the fall of 1993, I sing loudly and sway my arms, aching to get into the aisles and leap with the joy that I have found. I have not yet danced, but my resistance to hardcore worship is breaking down.

When I open my eyes, they inevitably fall upon one of three people worshipping in the aisles: a lady doing cartwheels; a curly-haired man pacing back and forth swinging his long, wiry arms and bobbing his head; and a tanned guy about my age with perfectly trimmed hair and earrings running up and down each ear. Mostly, I see this jeweled man. And it seems that everyone else sees him, too. He is a leaper and a spinner, and his shouts of "Hallelujah Jesus!" sail over the other voices and instruments. During the fastest songs, he jumps several feet off the ground and spins around and flails his arms like a tribal warrior. His name, Kaysie tells me, is Brandon. He is the leader of the Preppies. But he talks to everyone, as if he is the connective tissue between the various social groups. He knows everyone and everyone knows him, and I decide from afar that that this guy is living a grand life. He has God figured out and he has people figured out and he has a beautiful Christian girl at his arm. I assume he leads a Bible study and probably knows what the Book of Daniel means. But most important, he is a fantastic worshipper. I want to be like him because he is linked to the very heart of God.

There are other worshippers I admire, too. The worship services at the charismatic megachurch allow me to get to know everyone from afar. I see the outstanding worshippers and then sneak a peak at their not-worshipping lives before and after services. The cartwheeling lady has a hippie husband next to whom she stands closely and smiles; theirs are lives of intense spiritual satisfaction. The curly-haired bobber wears a Harvard sweatshirt and has surely exercised all that education in the service of sublime theology. As with Brandon, everyone talks to the curly-haired man. There is an older man in a brown suit who dances up and down the aisles waving a handkerchief each Sunday, a muscle-bound bald man and his big-haired wife who stand up stiffly at the very front of the church and grin, then walk about embracing people and praying in their ears. I imagine whole lives for all of these people: they know their Bibles backward and forward; they committed grave sins years ago and have been liberated once and for all; they share the gospel with their coworkers and classmates; everyone who comes into contact with them converts to Christianity; they rise early each morning and pray with confidence and read the Bible with absolute assurance.

I admire, even adore, these fellow Christians, and whether they know it or not they are teaching me how to know God. Regardless of the accuracy of the lives I imagine for them, they are teaching me how to worship, how to praise, how to dance.

It does not take me long to try worship dancing. Once I sing "I Believe in Jesus" and mean it in the pit of my soul, I am on a slippery slope of religious experimentation, and I land happily in a comfortable pool of worship. I have never been as excited about anything as I am about the idea that there is a God and He lived on Earth in the form of Jesus and Jesus was killed and then rose from the dead and those acts of death and resurrection mean that no matter what I have done I can be completely accepted by God and spend eternity basking in His love. Nothing about the story seems confusing. There is no occasion for doubt. It is a perfect picture of the meaning of life, and I imagine that the entire human race is slowly opening its eyes to that picture, too. Thinking through this puts springs on the bottom of my feet. It is cause for dancing and shouting. My joy for Jesus increases as I dance, not the other way around. I begin to dance to express my joy, but I am more joyous the more I kick my heels and wave my arms. I flirt with it for a few weeks, first standing in front of my chair and bouncing gently on my heels, then excusing myself into the aisle and jumping a little higher with the other dancers. In a remarkably short time, I go from being attracted to the beautiful liberation I see in Brandon and others to embracing that liberation for myself.

Self-consciousness falls away quickly in the charismatic megachurch. It is easy to believe that no one cares how you worship because everyone is so idiosyncratic and unashamed in their physical expression. We are a motley gathering of disparate improvisers, and we blend together into a kind of harmonious disunion. The man waving his arms in circles is no more ostentatious than the lady turning cartwheels. Sure, there are plenty of scoffers who stand off to the side, but I have been one of those scoffers too, and so has virtually everyone else. The feeling is that sooner or later the scoffers will be clearing their own space in the aisle so they too can spin and leap.

One Sunday, the worship levee gives way. I let it all hang loose. I cannot help it. I begin to dance and sing to God, coming ever-so-slightly off the floor, but soon realize that I am more joyful than my little jig can express. I need to do more. I begin to bounce-bounce-bounce-LEAP-bounce-bounce-bounce-LEAP. I push my body higher and higher into the air, laughing and shouting. God is so excellent! He is amazing! My heart fills to the brim with love for Him. "You're so good, God!" I shout, feeling His goodness trickle down through my soul. I am bad and He is making me good, and my gratefulness needs dancing to find full expression. Bounce-bounce-bounce-LEAP. Bounce-bounce-bounce-LEAP. I am unfettered. "JEEE-SUSSS!" rifles out of my throat. "JEEE-SUSSS!" at the very tip-top of my lungs. Everything in my body wants to express my devotion to God. The very Creator of the Universe, the God of the skies and water and galaxies, has come into my soul. It is a phenomenal incompatibility that God has chosen to transcend, and I am aware of it like being aware of the sun. I want to strip off all my clothes. I want to swing from the rafters. I want to high-five all three thousand members of the charismatic megachurch. I cannot, so I just dance as long and hard as I can.

This time, even when the fast-paced songs downshift to slow-paced songs, I keep on dancing. I have seen the curly-haired man do this before, and I know it is OK. If you are really, truly grateful to God, it does not matter how you express it, just as long as you do. No one minds if I keep leaping during the ballad "More Love, More Power." They know that my expression of joy has to come out so I won't pop.

I am exhausted and sweaty during the sermon. I already look forward to the next song service. Afterward, as I filter out of the church, Bible in one hand, car keys in the other, I feel a hand on my shoulder. "Hey man, I want to talk to you." I turn toward the voice and see Brandon. His hand remains on my shoulder as I face him, and he pulls me in toward his chest and gives me a giant hug. My arms hang limp at my sides. He pulls away but maintains his grasp on my shoulders. He looks me in the eyes. "I know you don't know me, but I just wanted to tell you what a blessing you are to me," he says. "I've been seeing you come in here for months now, and I've been watching you every week. I can tell that God is doing something in your life, and I can see that He has set you apart. I saw you dancing this morning, and you were so free. I just want to encourage you to seek Him and cultivate that freedom. He loves you a lot and I can tell He is getting ready to do great things in your life."

I nod. I smile. I say thanks. I cannot respond otherwise. I feel I am talking to the Pope. This is the most spiritually with-it man at the charismatic megachurch, and he is telling me that my worship dancing is a blessing to him. He has no idea. Suddenly, I want nothing more than to be his close friend, and to be friends with all the people at the charismatic megachurch. Forget solitude. I want to take up residence here.

4

Megachurch, Megafaith

My days are different, and so my life is different. How we spend our days, says Annie Dillard, is how we spend our lives. I am spending my life as a Christian. I listen to Christian music most of the time. I read Christian devotional material in the mornings and evenings. I am at the church several days a week, or else out on the town with new Christian friends. Our evening activities consist of things I would have thought boring and square a year ago: watching a PG-rated movie, eating pizza at Old Chicago, going out for ice cream. We also nearly always incorporate at least an hour of worship. Brandon brings his guitar everywhere, and on a moment's notice he will begin to play and we'll circle round and sing songs to God.

My new identity, connected as it is to my Southern Baptist memory, is fairly easy to slip into. It is enough like the Christianity I knew as a child that in some ways I feel I'm picking up where I left off before high school. But as the months go on, I gather that my new identity has several qualifications. I am a not a mere Christian. I am fancier. More complex.

I am Protestant, meaning I am not Catholic. I do not know exactly why I am not Catholic or what is wrong with being Catholic, but I suspect it has something to do with dead religion and Mary. Sometimes we talk of how Catholics need to know Jesus. I hear people say, "I am witnessing to a coworker of mine who is Catholic," and I do not question the assumption that Catholics are not Christians; I make it my own. I do not yet ascertain that the moniker *Protestant* is itself loaded with our non-Catholicism. It is pronounced

"*Prahtest*-ant" and not "*Protest*-ant," so I'm not immediately hip to the significance.

I am an evangelical. I assume this just means I support evangelism, and I do.

I am a charismatic and a Pentecostal. These terms account for the dancing and the tongue speaking, the prayers for healing and the prophecies. I'm not sure which term applies to which phenomenon—does speaking in tongues make me a charismatic and dancing in worship make me a Pentecostal, or is it the other way around? As it turns out, though there are squabbles about their distinctions, *charismatic* and *Pentecostal* are used more or less synonymously in the Christian circles I'll move in over the course of years to come. But I do not intuit this congruence early on, so for a while I think of myself as a Charismatic Pentecostal.

The pastor at the charismatic megachurch explains it all jokingly one Sunday. He grins out from the pulpit. "If anyone asks you what kind of church you go to," he says, "tell them it's a Protestant Evangelical church. No, a Protestant Evangelical Charismatic church. Wait, a Full-Gospel Evangelical Pentecostal church." Laughter ripples through the crowd. "No, let's call it a Protestant Evangelical Pentecostal Charismatic Full-Gospel church." Laughter. "We might also be fundamentalists, but don't tell anyone that." Laughter. "Oh, help me! Our identity is so confused!" he jokes. He is killing. Everyone is having a grand time. I laugh right along, but I don't really get the joke.

(The charismatic megachurch pastor has an uncanny knack for rendering the uncomfortable comfortable. This is a major part of his magnetic persona. He speaks the unspeakable and thereby makes it acceptable. We resist thinking of ourselves as schizophrenic Christians until he lets us know that that's OK. He'll joke from the pulpit about our fanaticisms, sometimes chiding us and sometimes approving. He paints a picture of the Christian life as flexible, adaptable, easygoing, but with a backbone of solid, foundational ideas. Whatever else it means to be a Christian, he is the kind of Christian I begin to want to be.)

"But come to think of it, many of you are Catholics, right?" Everyone looks around. This is surprising, especially among those of us who pray for Catholics to be saved. "How many of you went to Saturday evening Mass last night?" he asks. About one-fifth of the three thousand people raise their hands. "OK, then," says the pastor, "tell them this church is a Protestant Catholic tongue-speaking, clapping, shouting, absolutely thrilled about Jesus church!" Rapturous applause.

This means, as I take it, that we have fully realized Christianity. Everyone has varied pasts and ongoing affiliations, but on Sundays we come together to the charismatic megachurch to worship in spirit and in truth.

I apply all the signifiers of identity to myself. In my hearing, they are all capitalized, like *Christian*. There is a history to these terms, a story behind their coinage and usage, but that history is masked. As far as I can tell, we at the charismatic megachurch are doing what the first Christians did: believing in Jesus with all our hearts and trying to experience everything He has given us. This means speaking in tongues and praying for healing and casting out demons and prophesying and taking seriously all the supernatural stuff in the New Testament. I can see by the jumbo screens and rock 'n' roll worship that the charismatic megachurch has been fashioned by contemporary design, but that is all just packaging. What is inside—what happens in our hearts—is ancient Christian wisdom. What is happening to us is equal to what happened to the first Christians in Jerusalem in the first century A.D. Their experience is our experience. Being a Protestant Evangelical Charismatic Pentecostal Christian means being a Christian in the biblical sense, the true sense. This is Christian faith at its finest, faith as God intended. The Southern Baptists, the Lutherans, the Methodists, the Presbyterians—I see that they are Christians, too. They are on the right path, but they are walking awfully slowly.

In the coming years, my collage of adjectival names and titular nouns will become confused. Sometimes in charismatic prayer groups I will hear people praying that evangelicals would come to know God's power. And later, I'll hear noncharismatic evangelicals talking with disdain about charismatics, whom they consider outside the evangelical pale. I will wonder how anti-evangelical charismatics identify themselves, if not as evangelicals. I will wonder why the anticharismatic evangelicals think the charismatics are so fundamentally misguided when the groups are united on the most essential matters. I will understand why none of us want to be called a fundamentalist, even though that seems to be what we are.

Religious scholars and sociologists usually fare little better in sorting out these issues. The terms and their modifiers were not birthed cleanly, they say. It's hard to find the progenitors and say precisely which tradition applies to which term. As a result, we're left with a bastardized nomenclature. Many scholarly studies of modern Christianity begin with a guide to terms that pays attention to the shades of difference between, say, big *E* Evangelical and small *e* evangelical, or evangelical and fundamentalist. They choose to use certain definitions of each term for the purposes of their study, while admitting that in everyday Christian society the definitions slip and slide.

One need not read much history to discover that these terms all arise out of the same basic past. What distinguishes *my* kind of evangelical Protestantism (the charismatic kind) from my father's kind of evangelical Protestantism (the Southern Baptist kind) are varying degrees of historical hiccups and theological tiffs. If the church reforms of the sixteenth century, when Martin Luther challenged papal authority, represent the big divide between all things Catholic and all things not Catholic, the multiple thousands of Protestant denominations and movements are rooted in the same soil. Rock 'n' roll church music is a reverberation of Luther's "A Mighty Fortress Is Our God" (which, fittingly, was originally a drinking song and which, also fittingly, is rearranged into a rousing praise jig by the band at the charismatic megachurch). Even without knowing this, in my first year as a Christian it is possible for me to focus on the similarities, and not the differences, between my charismatic present and my Southern Baptist past. The senior pastor of the charismatic megachurch is always advising us to strive for Christian unity, likening the corporate Body of Christ to Baskin-Robbins. He loves all thirty-one flavors, he says, and though he prefers strawberry above all he knows the best ice cream sundaes feature several kinds of scoops.

Nevertheless, in the fall of 1993, being the kind of Christian that I am—and I'll stick with the blanket terms *evangelical* and *charismatic*—means a host of things culturally and ideologically that become clear to me quickly as the months progress. My beliefs are oriented around a few key issues: eternal salvation through faith in Jesus; the Bible's perfection, authority, and utter reliability; God's discernible action and presence in the world, especially through the gifts of the Holy Spirit such as speaking in tongues and prophecy; and my responsibility to be a part of the ongoing effort to share these ideas with everyone on the face of the planet. All this is eminently apparent, even obvious, to me and my charismatic megachurch friends. These notions and impulses fill our imaginations, direct our conversations, and guide the course of our days.

We are in good company. Churches like this charismatic megachurch are the fastest growing churches in the world. Currently, around four hundred American churches are megachurches, meaning they have two thousand or more congregants. Several are well beyond the ten thousand mark, and a handful reach upwards of twenty thousand. Some are charismatic, some are Presbyterian, some are more blandly nondenominational. All are conservative and lean toward literalist readings of the Bible.

The fact of these big churches may seem ordinary now, but they were an uncanny sociological surprise. Lots of religious-minded folk expended lots of twentieth-century energy worrying about how to make traditional spirituality relevant to the modern world (or, rather, how to protect it from being stained by the modern world), and lots of secular-minded folk expended similar energy predicting that piety just might crumble underneath advances in technology, capitalism, and contemporary philosophy. While these concerns (or hopes, depending on your perspective) about increased secularism occupied the pages of journals and books, megachurches flourished everywhere during the 1980s and 1990s, from Los Angeles to Louisville to Seoul. They are still flourishing.

The latest edition of the *World Christian Encyclopedia*, representing decades of research compiled by an international team of church demographers, paints a picture of Christianity growing by leaps and bounds, especially in the Southern Hemisphere. And the brand of Christianity that is most responsible for that growth is Pentecostalism. Outside of America, as sociologist Peter Berger has noted, 85 percent of all evangelicals are Pentecostal. Charismatic Christianity has been exploding for more than a century, and it is still on the rise. It is the fastest growing religious movement in the world.

Despite this vastness, Pentecostalism is still a dirty little secret within certain large segments of Christendom. Talk to a Presbyterian, or a Southern Baptist, or some manner of nondenominational Christian, or a liberal Congregationalist or United Methodist, or Catholic or Episcopalian or Eastern Orthodox. Talk to them about charismatic Christians and you may induce eye-rolling or gagging or pronounced skepticism. I have moved back and forth between charismatic and noncharismatic and Christian and non-Christian circles since 1993, and I often find that the non-Christians are more accepting of the notion of the charismatic experience than noncharismatic Christians are. Perhaps this is understandable: we charismatics have not always put our best foot forward. We have not set a good example. People think of us as televangelists and sandwich-board street preachers and big-tent revivalists who play with snakes and try to heal cancer with our bare hands. That is not who we are. But those versions of ourselves have occupied the public imagination because they make a lot of noise. Even when we do a good job of keeping our most embarrassing figures indoors, we are still an odd bunch with our dancing and prophesying and arm waving and tongue speaking. We are the freaks of Christianity. The uninitiated have good cause to be aghast, and even the initiated, like myself, can grow aghast all over again with a little distance. I have been aghast and un-aghast and re-aghast and back and forth and back again ever since the fall of 1993.

Halfway through that autumn, I am surprised to hit it off with a classmate named Ronny. I learn quickly that he is a Christian, and I'm happy to meet another believer outside of the walls of my own church. Ronny and I hang out a few times and I get the feeling that his faith is not as . . . well, *invigorating* as mine. I keep trying to talk about God. Ronny wants mostly to talk about sports and U2. Ronny eventually confesses to me that he is glad for my openness of faith, because his own faith has been on the back burner for some time. Ronny says he has been meaning to get his life straight for years. His problem is that he keeps having sex (*fornicating*, that is), and try as he might he is never able to resist the temptation. Ronny is tall and dark and built like a middleweight boxer, and I have no problem imagining his ample opportunities for temptation.

Ronny and I talk long and hard about all the things he already knows: God's love and forgiveness, and if you confess your sins He is faithful and just to forgive you of your sins and cleanse you of all unrighteousness. My suspicion is that Ronny could use something more: a nice, big dose of the charismatic megachurch and all the enthusiasm therein. His fire for God will surely be fanned by radical worship.

Ronny isn't sure about this. He was raised in the Church of Christ.

"So?"

"So," he explains, "the Church of Christ isn't big on praise and worship music."

"Right," I say, acting like I know what he's talking about. "But that's OK. You can just sit and listen."

"Well, but there's a band there, right?"

"Yeah."

"Like, a guitarist and a drummer and all that?"

"Sure. Of course. Why?"

"We don't believe in any of that."

I don't get it. How can you not believe in a band?

Ronny explains that it is dishonoring to God to have guitars and a drummer and a saxophonist in church. I am incredulous. How could God possibly be dishonored when we worship Him as loudly and boisterously as we do at the charismatic megachurch? Does He not love worship? Does He not tell us in the Bible to make a joyful noise? Yes, Ronny rejoinders, but should our worship take the form of "the world's" music? "You mean like U2?" I sneer. Ronny and I argue back and forth, our conversation taking a turn for the ecclesiological. We move from worship music to soteriology, and the gulf between his Jesus and mine widens. A few minutes ago, we were trading Scripture verses about sexual purity and forgiveness and Ronny was being counseled to recommit his life to Christ. Now, Ronny is flipping through the Bible to show me where it says that everyone who is not water-baptized is going to hell. I'm beginning to wonder if the Church of Christ is a cult, and I sense Ronny is wondering the same thing about my charismatic megachurch.

Before things become too heated, Ronny and I agree to leave our doctrinal differences aside. There are some matters we cannot understand, we say. Maybe we should visit each other's church. Graciously, Ronny decides to go first, and I pick him up the following Sunday night on the way to the charismatic megachurch.

We walk in just as the music is beginning to play. Ronny stiffens, but I am sure that once he sees the freedom we have in the Spirit of God, he won't be able to help but love our worship. How could he deny that God is present here? I'm excited, and a little nervous, to see what will happen. I do not expect Ronny to join us dancing in the aisle, and I tell him so as we walk toward our seats. He stiffens further. Had I not mentioned there would be dancing?

I show Ronny to a seat, and, as is my custom, slip off my sandals, take off my watch, and pull my keys and wallet out of my pockets. I like to be free of worldly accoutrements when I worship God. I tell Ronny to make himself at home, and I'll be in the back of the auditorium should he need me. He barely answers, his eyes glued to the jumbo screens. This is all so normal to me now that I'm amused at his distress. It may take a while, but he will come around. He will become infested with the excitement of God, and in the end this will help him get his life back on track.

Two songs into worship, I'm dancing and almost lost enough in the moment not to notice Ronny walking hurriedly by. I stop and look at him striding his way toward the hallway outside the auditorium. I wonder at him but don't chase him. I continue dancing and watching the door at the same time. He doesn't return after several minutes, so I walk into the hallway. No sign of Ronny. I look both ways and, through the windows on the church's front entrance, I notice him standing at the edge of the parking lot. I walk outside.

"What's up? You OK?"

"No. I think I'm gonna go home." He doesn't look at me. His eyes are fixed on the horizon.

"Go home? Really? Is this bothering you that much?"

"No, no. It's just, um, I got sick in there. I threw up in the bathroom."

"You threw up?" I begin to laugh, then stifle it. He looks as though he could puke again.

"Yeah, I don't, I don't know. I just, I felt nauseated and I went to the bathroom and everything came up."

"Was it because of the band?"

"No, no. I don't think so . . . I don't know."

"Well, do you want me to take you home now?"

"It's OK. I called my mom. She's coming to get me."

He called his mom? I'm ashamed, angry, and flummoxed all at the same time. Is Ronny so encumbered by his poor theology and deadening religiosity that he can't see past it? Will he ever come around, as I have?

Or is my church so fanatical that it can make someone throw up?

Ronny's mom soon arrives; she doesn't look at me through her car window. Ronny slides into the car and off they go.

The evening does not impair our friendship, but we never talk about that night. We even pray together a few times, but silently we agree to live with the major differences between our approaches to God. We are both Christians. We are both evangelicals, though I cannot see how Ronny will ever evangelize anyone with a church that won't play decent music. We believe in the same God, but we believe that we should believe in Him differently, and we are glued to those differences. His faith is stodgy and cold to me; mine is nauseating to him.

Privately, I am convinced that Ronny's problem is one of religion. *Religion* has become a bad word in my lexicon. I have come to think of many noncharismatic Christian groups as "religious" rather than "relational." I have a relationship with God. Ronny has religion. Catholics have religion. Southern Baptists have religion. Being a Protestant Evangelical Charismatic Pentecostal Christian means being unreligious. Religion is dead. Relationship is alive. Religion is a system of dull practices. Relationship is full-blooded, dynamic, *real*. Religious people don't worship God; they worship the form of God.

My charismatic friends and I often pray against the spirit of religion that is holding people captive to these old forms. This becomes confusing when I read Christian writers for whom the term *religion* had no negative connotation. When C. S. Lewis says, "If you are a Christian you do not have to believe that all the other religions are simply wrong all through," I wonder why he includes Christianity in the category of religion at all. I know some Christians are religious and therefore need to be refreshed in their relationship with God. But Lewis doesn't seem to imply that there is anything wrong with religion itself. I wonder if he too was deceived by the spirit of religion.

But doesn't ritual mean doing the same thing every week? And don't I do the same thing every week, even if that thing is as active and emotional as charismatic worship? I worry over this, and I try to incorporate surprise into my worship so that it does not become routine, which means ritualized, which means religious. I have read that sometimes in worship you should do whatever makes you the most uncomfortable. If you are comfortable, you may not be worshipping God; you may be only doing your routine. So I dance even when I don't feel worshipful. (Brandon and I always encourage one another with this: God deserves our worship whether we feel like it or not.) During the slow songs, I am most comfortable pacing and singing, so I try to sit in silence and just listen for God. I also do this in my room, alone, in the still of the morning. I consider the irony that sitting in silent meditation is a stolid religious practice for some; for me, it is the most discomfiting sacrifice of worship.

I understand why Ronny was ill at ease during our worship service—the size and volume of the worship band is enough to shock anyone who has not seen it before—but I feel strongly that his position on worship music is unbiblical. Psalm 150 says to "praise him with the sounding of the trumpet, praise him with the harp and lyre, praise him with tambourine and dancing, praise him with the strings and flute, praise him with the clash of cymbals." Sounds pretty festive to me, I think, smugly. We at the charismatic megachurch have trumpets, tambourines, and dancing in plenty, and there is a logical progression from harps and cymbals to electric guitars and drum kits. King David, I am sure, would have been at the forefront of the Christian music industry.

Indeed, the Bible offers explanations of my entire Christian experience. It is my sourcebook and my guide. In spite of Ronny and lingering doubts I have about the validity of portions of charismatic practice, I know what I am experiencing is authentic because the Bible tells me so.

The biblical explanation of my charismatic experience starts like this. Five books into the New Testament, we come to a book called the Acts of the Apostles. It is written by the same person who wrote the Gospel According to Luke, whom we call "Luke" because tradition and textual evidence suggest he wrote that gospel and also Acts. Luke is the most thoroughgoing historian of the gospel writers. He offers the fullest account of Jesus' life, and Acts is the only existing ancient history of the formation of the first Christian church. Acts opens with Jesus still hanging around after His resurrection, giving His disciples some final instructions and performing miracles here and there to prove that He is indeed the resurrected Lord. He then ascends to heaven, but not before reminding everyone to wait around for the Holy Spirit, who will be coming at any minute. "Don't go anywhere," He tells them. "The Holy Spirit is on the way." So they remain in Jerusalem and take care of a little business. Judas Iscariot, who set the crucifixion machine in motion when he fingered Jesus for the Roman authorities, has become riddled with guilt and commits a kind of hara-kiri (according to Luke, anyway; Matthew's gospel has Judas hanging himself). So the twelve-pack of apostles is one short. Peter gets everyone to agree to choose Judas's replacement, which they do by playing something like Rock-Paper-Scissors. Shortly after, while everyone is in town for the Festival of Pentecost, the Holy Spirit arrives as promised. They can't see it, but they can sure feel it. A wind blows about and tongues of fire come and lay down on top of them. They all begin to speak in other languages. They act like drunk men, but as Peter explains to the onlookers, it is only 9:00 A.M.; they haven't had time to drink yet. They babble away, only it is not babble at all; it is a multilingual conference. Jews from all over the Diaspora have come to Jerusalem for Pentecost, and each one can hear words being spoken in his native tongue.

That's the story according to Luke, and that's the explanation for my experience of God. The Holy Spirit fell on Jesus' first followers during Pentecost, so two millennia later, by virtue of praying for this Holy Spirit and speaking words I don't understand—"keilley onoomba shoktura"—I think of myself as a Pentecostal. Or a charismatic, because *charisma* means a divinely inspired gift or power. How *tongues* transitions from the miraculous ability to speak another known language to odd and unintelligible vocalizations is a little harder to explain, but I can find a biblical explanation for it too. At the charismatic megachurch, in fact, a specific biblical explanation is offered to me every Sunday morning.

From time to time during the song service, the band plays softly while the pastor allows someone to hold a microphone and share what is on her heart and mind. Sometimes this spiritually endeavoring person reads a Bible passage, sometimes she offers a prophecy (which is understood as God speaking through her to us), and sometimes she speaks in an unintelligible tongue for several minutes and then translates the gargle into English. This is a little odd, yes? Yes. The charismatic megachurch acknowledges this strangeness, putting a Bible verse of explanation on each of the three jumbo screens. When the prophesier or tongue speaker begins, the screens hold this passage:

> When you come together, everyone has a hymn, or a word of instruction, a revelation, a tongue or an interpretation. All these must be done for the strengthening of the church. If anyone speaks in a tongue, two—or at the most three—should speak, one at a time, and someone must interpret. 1 Corinthians 14:26–27

Or this:

> Two or three prophets should speak, and the others should weigh carefully what is said. And if a revelation comes to someone who is sitting down, the first speaker should stop. For you can all prophesy in turn so that everyone may be instructed and encouraged. 1 Corinthians 14:29–31

Or, perhaps most forcefully, this:

> Now about spiritual gifts, brothers, I do not want you to be ignorant. . . . Now to each one the manifestation of the Spirit is given for the common good. To one there is given through the Spirit the message of wisdom, to another the message of knowledge by means of the same Spirit, to another faith by the same Spirit, to another gifts of healing by that one Spirit, to another miraculous powers, to another prophecy, to another distinguishing between spirits, to another speaking in different kinds of tongues, and to still another the interpretation of tongues. All these are the work of one and the same Spirit, and he gives to each one, just as he determines. 1 Corinthians 12:1, 7–11

The charismatic megachurch, it seems, is doing church precisely as the Bible prescribes. When I look up these passages on my own at home, they lead to other passages, such as: "For anyone who speaks in a tongue does not speak to men but to God. Indeed, no one understands him; he utters mysteries with his spirit" (1 Corinthians 14:2). That explains the Tatooine sounds. It does not quite fit with tongues as described in the second chapter of Acts, but it does not contradict it either, and it certainly fits with my feeling about the sounds I utter when I try to speak in tongues: they are a mystery. I am grateful to the charismatic megachurch for pointing me toward these passages. I never read them in all my Southern Baptist Sunday School programs of yesteryear, and so now I feel that the charismatic megachurch is paying attention to more portions of the Bible than other churches. More Bible is better Bible.

My own personal tongue speaking retains an aura of uncertainty for a great while. In fact, there never is a time when I am completely sure that I can speak in tongues anytime and all the time. Many charismatics around me tell me that I should believe in my gift of tongues. The Holy Spirit guy who first tried to baptize me in the Holy Spirit, the one who told me that all professing Christians have this secret ability and that it is up to us to engage that ability, was offering a kind of party line. There is one school of charismatic doctrine that says that tongue speaking is only one of the many evidences of the baptism of the Holy Spirit, and that one should not look for it any more or less than for other things such as miracles of healing and prophecy. But the working assumption among many charismatics is that most of us can, and should, speak in tongues. When I make a meeting with another deacon to ask for advice on tongue speaking, he gives me the party line too. If you're a believer, he says, you've got the gift. You just gotta exercise it. Open your heart to God and the Holy Spirit will pray through you, will speak out of you. All Christians can speak in tongues, he says; they just don't know it yet. It's like when you move into a new house and the utilities department has to turn your electricity on so you can use it; the Holy Spirit just had to turn on tongues, and now you can use it.

Don't think too much about this issue, he assures me. Just practice it. God has given you the gift of tongues. Just believe it and do it.

I am in a different place in the fall of 1993 from where I was ten months earlier. I don't gurgle sounds and then go smoke pot. I speak in tongues with faith. It feels wonderful even though it is mingled with slight uncertainty. I find more scriptural confirmation of my experiences, hints that Jesus said things to a small group of people in the Middle East two thousand years ago that are coming true in my life today. "Whoever believes in me," he said, "as the Scripture has said, streams of living water will flow from within him." John's gospel quotes Jesus as saying this in chapter 7, verse 38, and then glosses it: "By this he meant the Spirit, whom those who believed in him were later to receive." This resonates with me because speaking in tongues feels like water bubbling up from within and pouring out of my mouth. Sometimes I shout in tongues. Sometimes I sing. The sounds are absolute nonsense to my mind, but only to the part of my mind that is listening for English. To another part, a part that has more significance, a part that is listening for eternal truth, for connection to the larger cosmos, for adherence to God no matter if it makes sense, the sounds are musical. It is better, in fact, that they do not make sense. If they made sense, they might be a product of myself. Since they do not, they might be a product of that which is beyond myself.

My tongue prayers are strengthened by experiences of praying with other Christians. Prayer Warriors is a group that meets every Tuesday night. This is a meeting for the seriously committed believer. Who else would take an entire evening in the middle of the week to go to someone's house not to talk, not to eat, not to drink, not to watch a movie, but only to pray? We walk through the door at 6:00 P.M. and set to business. A CD of praise music is played, which sets the mood and suggests the tone for our task: praying long and praying hard. We pray for lots of things, but mainly we either glorify God or cry out against Satan. We pray that people do not go to hell, but to heaven. We pray His kingdom come, His will be done. His kingdom come, His will be done. This means that people will be saved from their sins and the inevitable consequences of those sins, both eternal and temporal. It means that people will be suddenly, miraculously healed of diseases, or else that doctors will have wisdom in nurturing them to health. It means that drug dealers will be thwarted, that pornography stores will close, that child molesters will be caught. All such things are demonic schemes, products of darkness. We pray that light will shine through the darkness and overcome it.

We are doing good. We are praying actively, not passively. We call this Spiritual Warfare, going to battle against unseen powers with invisible armor. Bad things happen in the world because Satan is the prince of the earth; so we read in John 12:31. We know that the true battle for the Christian is against Satan's kingdom and his unseen legion of demons that wreak havoc upon human lives; so we read in Ephesians 6:12. Prayer is our powerful weapon. Prayer hurts Satan. We come together to hurt him, to spoil his plan. We come together to bind the powers of darkness and loose the powers of goodness, for whatever we bind on Earth is bound in heaven, and whatever we loose on Earth is loosed in heaven; so says Matthew 16:19.

We do this not by sitting in a circle and taking turns praying out loud. Nor do we take a knee and pray silently within ourselves. As during worship services at the charismatic megachurch, this prayer group is a display of united idiosyncrasy. Some sit Indian-style on the floor, their heads hanging to their chests, praying softly in English or in tongues. Some sit on couches and chairs, leafing through their Bibles or kicking their heads back, eyes closed and lips moving in intercession. One man stands in the corner, facing the wall, arms raised slightly, hands shaking. He bounces a bit on his heels and nods his head up and down. Most of us pace. We walk in circles around the room. We walk up and down the stairs. We map out a small space, a ten-or-twelve-foot line and walk back and forth, back and forth. We march in prayer. Movement keeps our minds active. It is a cultural habit rooted in charismatics' desire to simply stay awake, to pray fervently for long hours. Pray without ceasing, the Bible says. We are doing our best to try.

The sound of group prayer is much like the sight of group worship—varied, cacophonous. Prayers are whispered in English, shouted in tongues, or whispered in tongues and shouted in English. It doesn't matter. Some sing loudly to God or bind the devil with furious yelps. Usually, Prayer Warriors begins with little sound save the music, but as the evening progresses the volume of prayer increases. The Spirit is stronger the longer we pray, the louder we pray. But not always; sometimes the Spirit seems stronger in silence. We try to detect these differences and let them lead us. Most often, the last twenty minutes or so of Prayer Warriors is a loud, violently joyous affair. We get our best work done in these times. Finally, when it all seems to be over—and this is sometimes at 8:00, sometimes at 9:00, sometimes at 10:00, but usually about 7:30—the prayer leader lifts his voice above the rest and closes with a few final words of prayer. Amen.

Prayer is our primary way of changing the world, helping humanity. It is a rush, an utter thrill to serve people this way. No one knows we are doing it. We are keeping it humbly to ourselves. We are not bothering anyone or pushing our beliefs into their faces. We are not picketing abortion clinics. We are not flinging hyperbolic dogmatic slurs at sinners on the streets. We are not the conservative Christian demagogues of talk radio. We are in private closets of prayer, serving God, desperately hoping that good things will happen on the Earth. No one knows we are here. We just do it for the good of humankind.

We Protestant Evangelical Charismatic Pentecostal Christians are changing the whole world, and no one knows it but God.

5

Go Ye Therefore

I am not sure how my experiences in the church are meant to inform my experience of the world outside church. I know I am meant to be a Christian publicly. Jesus' admonition to be outspoken (as I take it) at once challenges and haunts me: "Whoever acknowledges me before men, I will acknowledge before my Father in heaven. Whoever disowns me before men, I will disown before my Father in heaven." A couple of my old high school friends rap my basement room window from time to time. I answer, and they say, "Come on, let's go get stoned" or "You holdin'?" and I say, "Naw," and play it cool and they eventually leave. I always mean to say, "I can't because I've given my life to Jesus Christ" but can never force the words out of my mouth. I am a bit embarrassed to have come so clean so quickly, and, well, I do miss the smoking and the long, lackadaisical afternoons it promoted, the muted togetherness in grassy parks or black-lit basements.

My friendships with all but my closest high school mates have dissipated sans the stick-um of drugs and alcohol. Other than Ronny, I have few acquaintances at my university—commuter campuses do not offer much camaraderie—but two part-time jobs provide some company. The good employees at the County Seat clothing store in Chapel Hills Mall and Josh 'n' John's Ice Cream in downtown Colorado Springs are the first to meet with my Christian fervor. I start working at both these places during the school year, and I soon learn that being a Christian means relating to fellow employees differently than I did before. I have been working since age fourteen, and jobs were always a chance to be away from home and nearer to the world's escapades. In junior high, Chick-fil-A offered late-night make-outs with nineteen-year-old girls. Through high school, Target opened doors to new cliques of part-time college students whose apartments were filled with constant supplies of Corona and pot. And at AT&T, where I worked as a long distance operator in the summer after I graduated from high school, I could be fired with the grace of anonymity if caught being stoned at work—our cubicles and headsets ensured that we rarely ventured past "'Tsup?" and "See ya."

Now, employee relations are one more way in which life has been made new. My coworkers are not people with whom to smoke and drink and make out; they are not people to ignore; they are people who, like me, need God. They are fellow travelers in life, and they have taken the wrong road, and their misdirection has eternal consequences. I need to nudge them in the right direction. I need not only to get along but to be inspiring, to be set apart by what I believe, and be respected for that set-apartness. I need to share Jesus with them. "Go ye therefore" is my new motto.

This, to be sure, is an entirely new experience of human interaction.

I am not pushy about Jesus, and I do not expect my fellow employees to kneel at the register and make a confession of faith. In fact, it always seems that it is they, not I, who bring up the subject of Christianity in the first place. But I am blamed, in a good-natured manner, for all the God-talk that is happening among the staff at both jobs. I keep referencing God in nonspecific ways that force the conversation in that direction. For instance, I have (temporarily, as it turns out) dropped all swear words from my vocabulary. The folks at County Seat and Josh 'n' John's are quick to notice that these verbal placeholders are missing from my speech. This is enough to out me as a believer in Jesus before I've said anything about church or God.

"Patton, I've noticed you never cuss," my manager at County Seat says after my first couple weeks on the job.

"Yeah," I reply. "I guess I don't. I sure used to all the time." It's true that I have not really tried to stop cussing. The words have just disappeared.

"Why not anymore?" she asks. "Did you get religion?" Guffaw.

"Yeah, kinda," I say. "I just became a Christian."

"Oh," she says. ". . . that's cool . . ."

But then we talk about it. For hours. In detail. Religion opens up deep pockets of conversation. We talk about God and His will and death and the afterlife and where did the Bible come from and what about all the other religions and what is Jerry Falwell's problem and I had a friend who was a real preachy Christian but then he got this girl pregnant and totally ditched her—what kind of a Christian would do that?

I don't know the answers to many of my fellow employees' questions. I have not yet discovered apologetics and its mixed bag of responses. Mostly, I listen. They seem to think I am interesting to talk to, but I feel that I add little to the conversation. My coworker Sara has a friend visit one night, and she introduces me with, "This guy is interesting as shit to talk to." I shrug, not feigning modesty but knowing that all I've done is let Sara bend my ear with her staunch atheism. Being a Christian, and being open but not pushy about it, means that work conversations can be about more than gossip, more than sports, more than the price of gas. Everyone seems to like having found someone with whom they can discuss meaningful abstractions.

A fellow scooper at Josh 'n' John's Ice Cream mentions having seen the massive Jesus billboards that recently popped up around town. The charismatic megachurch has begun an advertising campaign on the city's highway billboards. "Depressed? Lonely? Anxious?" the billboards ask. Then, in big block letters, "JESUS is the answer!"

"Have you seen those things?" fellow scooper Jake asks.

"Yeah, I know those."

"What the hell are those people thinking?"

Well, I explain, as it turns out, I was at that church on Sunday, Jake, and I met someone who came just because he thought the billboard was a sign from God.

No pun intended.

I should have intended it. Jake laughs uproariously. I recover, swallow, remind myself not to take it too seriously because Jake is depraved and does not know any better.

Over time, I learn that all my fellow employees have very firm opinions about God and the Meaning of Life. One is a lapsed Mormon who is quite committed to her religious upbringing—as a set of ideas, as opposed to a set of practices. She talks the talk and hopes that someday she will walk the walk, but being lapsed works for her, for now. One is a Christian Scientist who, by all accounts, is also deeply committed but thinks that his feelings about God are best left unsaid at work. Still, he manages to explain at length that being a Christian has little to do with what one can and cannot do, or heaven and hell, or even prayer. I have a hard time seeing in what sense he is a Christian, and he has a hard time with my hard time. One of my County Seat managers is a scholarly agnostic who has lived the most moral life of any of us. She feels that the world is basically neutral and one has to work things out for oneself.

No matter which employee I work with at which job, we inevitably talk about God at some point during each shift. Our conversations are not outright attempts to convert one another to our thinking, though I secretly feel that I need to convert these people, and perhaps they secretly feel they need to convert me. While I skirt around the issue of conversion (*Would you like to make a decision for Christ tonight?*) we manage to argue for hours amidst the piles of blue jeans and t-shirts, or ice cream and waffle cones, as the case may be.

I have intuited that being a Christian means being pro things like Life, and anti things like Homosexuality, and these subjects often come up. I have not spent five minutes of good thought on any of these issues, much less five minutes good prayer, and rather than sophisticated opinions I have something more like matter-of-factness. I lose every argument that we have on these topics. Rather, I concede that I do not know enough to argue persuasively. "But I believe in God," I say, steering the conversation toward what I take to be the primary matter. "And I believe He knows the answers to these things. And I think He has an opinion about the way we live our lives."

They agree. If there is a God, He (or She, they add) has an opinion about our lives. But they have a different opinion of His opinion.

The conversations never become heated. I emphasize that Christianity is about love and forgiveness, and I hope they will see the truth of that someday so that they do not go to hell. (This is hard to say without shoving my tongue right through my cheek—I find it easiest to feign irony about fire and brimstone—but I try to say it because I believe it to be urgently true.) They tell me they also hope they do not go to hell. And they say that maybe they will check out my church sometime. I admit that I am a little scared for them to do this; it's a pretty wild place. But they are welcome anytime.

Being a Christian means I am not invited out drinking. It means people apologize when they say "goddam." Oddly, it also means I am called upon to pray when bad things happen in their lives ("Patton, I know you pray and stuff, so maybe you could say one for me because . . ."). It means that my relationships at work are not really relationships outside of work. I cannot think of what I would do with these people if we were not folding clothes and ringing registers. I cannot imagine that they would want to come to Prayer Warriors with me. Without fully realizing it, I have assimilated myself into a different society so firmly, so exclusively that I hardly know how to be apart from that society. But I am trying. What does it mean to be a friend to someone who does not believe what I believe? If my first and most important assessment of someone is that he or she is going to hell, how should I proceed to relate? What responsibility do I have? Is it ever OK to just be friends, to go to movies and coffee shops and enjoy their company without bringing up Christ? If I do that, and they never become Christians, will their blood be on my hands? Will I bear the responsibility for their eternal damnation?

I turn to the Bible, and the waters there are murky. The Apostle Paul is particularly hard to figure. "Do not be yoked with unbelievers," he says. "For what do righteousness and wickedness have in common? Or what fellowship can light have with darkness?" (2 Corinthians 6:14). Another time he writes, "It is shameful even to mention what the disobedient do in secret" (Ephesians 5:12). Then again, he also says, "Be wise in the way you act toward outsiders; make the most of every opportunity. Let your conversation be always full of grace, seasoned with salt, so that you may know how to answer everyone" (Colossians 4:5–6). I put all Paul's admonitions side by side and try to determine what God thinks about my interactions with my coworkers. How does all this translate into my life? What does it mean to go ye therefore? Do I need to be going ye everyday, in every possible moment? What if I have tried going ye and they have rejected it? Do I give them another chance? Should I remain friendly? Or should I shake the dust of the County Seat off my feet, as Jesus advised his disciples to do when their teaching was rejected in the towns of Judea?

As confused as I am about interacting with unbelievers, I am clear on their desperate need for Jesus. I see the influence of the devil in all of their lives, even the good ones. If I do not know quite how to interact with them in person, I do know how to pray.

In the neighborhood near my old high school, there is a tall, rocky, windy bluff that overlooks the city. Many nights I climb the bluff, walk to its edge, and survey the city lights. In high school, we'd come to get high. Now, I come to pray: for coworkers, for friends, for family, for the world. I sit and look across the city for a long while, to the south with the Broadmoor resort nestled into the Pike's Peak foothills, the scar of its old ski slope still etched into the mountain. To the north is the Air Force Academy, where our nation's best and brightest prepare for exemplary military careers. In between is one suburban development after another. It looks peaceful enough. From here, the strip malls sleep, the cars creep, the houses flicker with televisions and porch lights. A bustling sprawl filled with good people making good livings and raising good kids. From here, that is the way things look.

I know better. I know Satan is trying to mess the whole thing up. I know the town is filled with junior high kids like me, learning about sex through late-night porn on HBO. I know there are high schoolers like me, sneaking around and leaving trails of lies and stolen beer and close calls with the cops and let's call those eighth grade chicks we met. I know their deception. I know what their parents don't know, what their parents would be ashamed to know. I know, in fact, that it isn't even entirely their fault, that sin fills their hearts without their even knowing it.

And I know how to pray. I stretch my hands toward the city. Father, in the name of Jesus, loose Your Holy Spirit upon this land. Let love and forgiveness reign. Let Your kingdom come to Colorado Springs.

• • •

But there is also this: I am not always as committed a Christian as this account makes me out to be. On many of those windy bluff prayer vigils, I begin on my knees or fully prostrate in the dirt, seeking forgiveness for myself before I seek it for the city. I kneel until my knees are damp with blood, until pebbles stick deep into my palms. I'm so heavy with sin that I can't—won't let myself—get up.

My relationship with God is based on hunger. Sometimes I am starving. Other times I am sated. When I am hungry, prayer is invigorating and the Bible is a red-hot read. When I am full, prayer is a chore and ten verses take ten years. I have only been a zealous Christian for a few months now, but some days I wonder at my lack of growth. Why do I not know God more? Why do I still sin? Why do I not have more wisdom? Why do I not have more faith?

My prayers and Bible reading and worship dancing fill only so many hours of the day. In the rest of the hours I strive to maintain a heightened sense of spirituality, but frequently fail. I try hard to create a holy lifestyle, and I often feel like it's happening in spite of myself, but on my worst days I want to reject the whole package so I can have one evening with my old friends sitting and drinking and watching porn and having a good dirty time. Sometimes, I want to get high so bad I can smell the sweet smoke. I want to take a break from thinking about Paul's letter to the Romans and learning about justification and election.

And one time (that fall), I do.

When my high school chums return for the Thanksgiving holidays, Matt and I throw a three-day party in his mom's apartment while she is away. Matt has progressed in his own Christian faith, but he's not above partying. I am—or am trying to be. I behave myself for two parties straight, standing around and smoking cigarettes just to give my hands something to do, talking about old times and using all my available energy to resist the pot and beer.

But at the third party, the smoking circle in the kitchen smells so good and looks so fun and easy, and when my buddy Dan turns and catches my eye, lifts his head and looks at me as if to say, You sure you don't want a hit? I think, No, I am not sure, and I walk toward the kitchen without letting myself think about God about dancing about all the hours of prayer and reading Paul's letters; I push it all aside so easily so simply so forcefully and stride toward the circle and break in and say too coolly Can I get a hit and Dan says Right on and I take a long pull and the smoke fills my lungs and I feel fine. I hit again and again. I walk back to the couch. I make out with the girl I have been eyeing all night. I feel like I am getting a taste of who I was before, who I was six months ago, who I was before I abandoned myself to God.

The "What the hell have I done" and "Oh God I am so sorry" comes well before I am down from the high. It comes even as I am kissing, even as I am laughing, even as I am enjoying the company of my friends. As the party winds down, I so want to be home in my room where so much prayer has happened. I am safe there. I am godly there. I hate that I have smoked pot. I want to turn the clock back and do the evening over again. This time, I would just enjoy seeing my friends. That would be enough. This time, I would not worry what they think of me and why my habits have changed. This time, I would not need to smoke cigarettes to keep occupied. I would remember that my satisfaction and my security come from God, not from friends and not from pot.

As I drive home, I am too ashamed to apologize to Jesus, so I apologize to the Apostle Paul. I am sorry for trampling on his teaching. I do believe in what you said in Romans, Paul. I'm grateful for what you've taught me there. There is no condemnation for those who are in Christ Jesus.

Then I realize that praying to Paul is probably some kind of heresy, and I am doubly ashamed. Sin has clouded my spiritual judgment.

I inch back toward God over the course of several days, crying in prayer and weeping in worship. Not only did I lust and have an unsober mind and commit hypocrisy, but I lost an opportunity to witness to my friends. I had a chance to share Jesus with them, and instead they shared sin with me.

I pledge to fast and pray and read my Bible more. I need to be built up in Christ. I need a bigger dose of God so that I will not do such things. I need Christian training. I need more than church three times a week and Prayer Warriors and daily Bible study. I need an environment that will sharpen me full-time, that will teach my mind and heart and surround me with opportunities to be like Jesus. I need to find a place, a lifestyle, a system that will help me become the man of God I want to be. How can I make this happen?

I know the answer because I have been thinking toward it all along. It has been in the back of my mind for weeks. I've been wondering if I could find a way to make it happen, and now I am motivated, because I see that it may be my only hope.

I need to go to Oral Roberts University.

• • •

I am a freshman in college, but I do not feel the way a freshman should feel, and I know it. My friends from high school are meeting new people and living in dorm rooms, and though I am glad to be away from the ubiquitous drinking and pot and promiscuity, I am missing out on the canonical college experience. As a senior in high school, I meant to go to the University of Alabama because I lived in Alabama as a child and the Crimson Tide had just won the football championship. I applied and was accepted but could not pay the high out-of-state tuition. I procrastinated otherwise and missed the deadline for the good in-state schools. My parents encouraged me to stay home and attend the University of Colorado at Colorado Springs, a commuter extension of CU-Boulder. I agreed, with chagrin, to do so, on the understanding that I would stay only one year.

Most everything in my life has changed, but my resolve to leave home and attend university has not. Now that I am a full-fledged

Christian, I have a bubbling suspicion that I need to attend a Christian university. And soon after I become friends with charismatic Christians, I know exactly which Christian school I want to attend. Virtually every Christian of college age I have met in recent months matriculates at Oral Roberts University, which is in Tulsa, Oklahoma. If they do not go there initially, they transfer there. If they do not graduate from there, they begin there. It is the de facto college of choice for charismatic evangelicals, no matter their academic discipline.

I know Oral Roberts, the preacher, only from his notoriety in newspaper headlines and on bumper stickers. His story was the first in the string of televangelist scandals in the 1980s. There was Jim Bakker, the swindler with the wild sex life; and Jimmy Swaggart, the john who blubbered his repentance on national television. But first there was Oral Roberts, who in 1987 locked himself in something called a Prayer Tower and said that God was going to take him away if he did not raise $8 million by a certain date. As the deadline approached, the money came in under the wire, mostly from one devoted follower in Florida, but the dramatic intensity of the media frenzy paled only in the glare of the other televangelist controversies.

I had thus long assumed that Oral Roberts was a crazy man or a crook. But as I meet ORU students my notions of Oral are revised. He is not insane or even manipulative, they say. He was and is a powerful minister of God. Yes, he had an awful moment, but he had a long, admirable public career as an evangelist before the scandal, second only to Billy Graham. His school had a fantastic reputation before the financial woes. There's more good than bad to him, and ORU is still a solid school. This is the word among my charismatic friends.

Kaysie's boyfriend-and-shortly-thereafter-fiancé, Mark, graduated from ORU and took a job in Tulsa, and now Kaysie will be moving to Tulsa and living down the street from the campus. It doesn't take her long to hint that ORU might be the place for me, and it doesn't take me long to agree. My second semester at UCCS has begun, and I am already looking forward to the summer, to being away from the commuter school, to having a real college experience at a real college, and to being at a place where everyone wants to be like Jesus.

ORU hosts a College Weekend where students-to-be can visit, attend classes, and investigate funding. Kaysie encourages me to sign up for it, and I do. Brandon does too, and one night in late winter we rendezvous with ten other prospective ORU students and pile into a van for the eleven-hour drive through eastern Colorado, across the Kansas plain, and down into northeastern Oklahoma.

My expectations for the school are probably outsized, but the experience of arriving on campus for the first time might be deflating for even the most sobered traveler. ORU is to architecture what *The Brady Bunch* is to television; its most overwhelming feature is its date stamp. The desire to build symbolically Christian structures has combined with an unfortunate architectural era to create a kind of gaudy futurism: curved white-and-gold buildings representing the wholeness of man, star-shaped buildings suggesting the Star of David, three-sided structures symbolizing God's triune nature, and so on. ORU's unique architecture made it one of Oklahoma's leading tourist attractions for several years after it was built in the 1960s, but though architectural tastes change constructed architecture cannot; the campus now stands as a reminder of the styles of yesteryear, like a perpetual VH1 special.

We approach ORU from the front entrance at 777 South Lewis Avenue—a holy address because seven is a holy number, like twelve (tribes of Israel, disciples) and forty (days and nights). Pulling in, we see the welcoming structure: a forty-foot bronze statue of two hands clasped in prayer. "There's the Praying Hands," someone says, alerting me to the statue's apt name. The hands are pointed upward so that their wrists form the base and their rounded fingertips form the summit. Everyone in the van becomes quiet at the sight of this megalith, and I wonder whether we are all thinking *Wow, what a moving symbol of our faith*, or *Wow, what a misguided caricature*. I am stuck in between. I am committed to prayer—I am, in fact, a Prayer Warrior—but *this*. This is eccentric. Finally, some-one emits a snicker, and we all relieve ourselves with giggles. It's not blasphemous to laugh at the laughable. Really, it's a good-natured giggle at our own expense, because it is faith like ours that results in statues like this.

Driving past the Praying Hands, down a winding driveway that takes us to the campus parking lot, I am struck in particular by two structures rising above the trees: a cluster of three golden towers, and a giant space needle at the center of campus. The tower com-plex is called the CityPlex Towers. Originally named the City of Faith, it was the realization of Roberts's decades-long dream of a state-of-the-art medical complex. He intended the three buildings to house a 777-bed hospital, a diagnostic center, and a medical re-search center. Oral wanted his university to be adjacent to the best medical facility in the nation, like Johns Hopkins with prayer. Oral thought of modern medicine and prayer as two streams of healing that could bring spiritual and bodily restoration to an entire gener-ation, and he dreamed a noble dream of making the sick well en masse at the City of Faith. But the construction was prohibitively expensive, and the story of those expenses is the story of ORU's economic derailment. The project ultimately failed, and the med-ical towers precipitated President Roberts's debt relief campaign that made national headlines.

The other striking structure is where the campaign was housed: in a needle at the very center of campus called the Prayer Tower. The top of the tower holds a rotunda with a circumferential view of the campus and Tulsa's sprawl, and it was in this rotunda that Oral held himself captive. The exterior of the rotunda features sharp beams jutting out all around, meant to recall a crown of thorns. The tower's tip encases an ever-burning flame. At the base is a visitor center and an Oral Roberts biographical museum, called the Journey Into Faith. Also located within is the operating center for ORU's twenty-four-hour prayer hotline, the Abundant Life Prayer Group. Operators are standing by for intercession requests around the clock.

We park and walk from building to building, gawking. The dormitories feature more right angles and jutting precipices than a teetering game of Jenga. The cafeteria looks capable of lifting off and spinning into the stratosphere. The general classroom building, named the Learning Resources Center, is a protruding diamond with twelve water drains, one for each apostle. It is surrounded with thin, sleek pillars meant to remind us of King Solomon's temple. Originally, it was as futuristic inside as its exterior suggests. The U.S. Department of Higher Education gave ORU a grant to make the LRC library an ultramodern laboratory of learning. RCA designed a kind of central nervous system that controlled a multi-media educational environment giving students immediate access to individual films and videos. Educators from around the world flew to Tulsa to gape with envy, and the Ford Foundation called the LRC "the most innovative facility of its kind."

Near the Prayer Tower is a chapel with reflective sides, called Christ Chapel. The building lurches up from the ground, representing the tents Oral used in revivals, and is supported with angling white arches that are supposed to evoke more praying hands. The interior is massive, with seats enough for thirty-five hundred undergraduate and graduate students, plus faculty. An immense, underused pipe organ inhabits the front quarters. A stage extends out from in front of the organ, and everything else is sloping floor theater seating complete with cushioned folding chairs.

My head spins as we walk around and talk about the architecture and history of ORU. However odd everything looks now, there is a certain impressiveness of intention. Oral Roberts dotted every *i*, crossed every *t*, and his ingenuity and progressiveness command respect. But what to think in light of the financial scandal—which is, sadly, the moment most everyone knows from Oral's life? I remind myself not to suspect that Oral's misstep points toward some systematic or foundational problem. It was a misstep, and that is all. ORU is a place where saints are trained, and it needs to be kept safe from further scandal.

I frame my questions carefully. How did the school survive such a blow? Is Oral OK? I am assured that it is all in the deep and distant past. I learn that Oral's son, Richard, has taken the presidential reigns and restored order to the campus—financial, academic, and spiritual. President Richard will be telling us more about this later when he greets prospective students. ORU is not a school of the past, I am told. It is a school of the future.

And yet, beyond the recent past of the Prayer Tower incident, there is a past of golden days. While ORU was being designed and built, it was all the rage. Oral faced ridicule when he announced in the early 1960s that he intended to parlay his tent revival success into an academic enterprise, but the critics were silenced as the school achieved a quick aura of respectability. A demanding curriculum was designed, featuring an intensive study of Western civilization that required several semesters to complete. Ads were placed in *Sports Illustrated* and *Life*. Graduate schools were planned. No stone was left unturned. Even the men's basketball team was a formidable Division I force during the 1970s. Against the odds, Oral Roberts formed a community of scholars that shared his vision of combining Pentecostal passion with intellectual fortitude. Somehow, he was able to put together a faculty of professors who had received both doctorates *and* the baptism in the Holy Spirit.

By the time I arrive, no one is bragging about academic excellence; or at least, that is not the primary reason any of us is here. I have hardly inquired about academics, nor will I as I go through the application process. The way I see it, students come to ORU primarily to draw close to God. The riskiest thing about attending this school is not a loss of respectability of the academic or professional kind, but of the social. The more we walk around and the more we talk about the layout of the school, the more ORU's aesthetic is troubling just because it is so culturally backward. I worry about how I will see this later. Will I be a proud alum? Will I ever be piously motivated by these structures? Does it matter if I believe that I am called here? Probably not. It will be a hard calling in some ways, but I should be glad to take some blows for my faith.

Brandon and I do our best to laugh innocently at ORU's appearance. We agree that it should not much matter. The school buildings are merely a record of the tastes of their time. I'd rather be roaming among the marvelous stone structures in Boulder, but those are mere aesthetics. As with the charismatic megachurch, it is what is offered inside that counts. I do not care about the things of this world, I remind myself. I do not care about appearances. I am focused on matters of higher import.

Indeed, for the bulk of my weekend visit, the buildings are genuinely overshadowed by the people who walk among them. The grounds become hallowed for me as my admiration grows for the godly students receiving godly training. I stay in a (generous) student's dorm room and think him smart and kind and passionate for God. I visit a class and find it boring but bearable. I eat in the cafeteria. I play volleyball in the gym and dream with Brandon of winning the school's two-on-two tourney next year (we will place fourth; Brandon will blame officiating). I attend meeting after meeting on enrollment and financial aid and extracurricular activities and summer mission trips abroad. I see a thousand pretty girls in their skirts and dresses and large groups of cool guys in their collared shirts and ties—there is a dress code—and dream of dating the prettiest girls and befriending the coolest guys. I do all these things under the guise that I am *considering* ORU as my institution of higher learning, but there is never a shard of doubt. I will come here. God has called me here. Oral Roberts University is the place where I will become the man of God that God has called me to be.

I know this because we all know this. ORU is a place for radicals, for zealots, for Jesus freaks. Our devotion is front-and-center. At ORU you can pray long prayers over your breakfast and no one will think you strange. You can read your Bible on the bench outside. You can blare Christian rock unashamedly from your Jeep. You can kneel in a sudden fit of worship and no one will sneer—in fact, they may join you in prostration. Everyone is thrilled at the prospect of attending ORU because it is a charismatic monastery. Here, you can be devoted to God with everything you've got; such devotion is the point. At the charismatic megachurch, we prayerwalk and dance in worship and shout in tongues. At ORU, we will do all that in chapel twice a week, plus Sundays, and in the fellowship of other young Christians like us. Iron will sharpen iron. Our faith, already strong, may not be radically redefined here, but it will be strengthened while we study for accreditation in medicine or theology or English literature or pastoral youth ministry or political science. We will enroll as zealots and graduate as zealots with bachelor's degrees.

At the evening service on our second night in Tulsa, we are treated to praise and worship songs by the ORU worship band. The band is fantastically good; they play many of the same songs played at the charismatic megachurch, but with even more oomph. Brandon and I bolt from our seats, go down to the very front, just below the stage, and dance our hearts out before God and all the potential ORU students. Some of them join us. We have a raucous worship, hopping and shouting our praise in our usual way. We're excited about God in the way we're always excited about Him, but we're especially excited tonight. We know we'll spend countless hours in the coming years right here at the front of this chapel. This golden carpet, these golden chairs, this sloping chapel floor (which makes dancing a bit awkward) will be our holy temple of praise, our discipleship factory, our threshing floor on which the wheat of our hearts will be separated from the chaff. Whatever needs to be refined in us will be refined at ORU.

The final event of the weekend is a miniservice in the Baby Mabee, a smallish auditorium in ORU's ten-thousand-plus-seat Mabee Center. We squeeze into the room with several hundred other prospective students and some faculty. Richard Roberts and his ministry team sit near the front. We sing praise and worship songs for fifteen minutes, and then President Roberts goes onto the platform and sits on a stool to give a short informal talk. He reminds us what a wonderful place ORU is—how it has been, from its inception, an institution that takes both academics and spirituality seriously. He admits that there have been rough waters in the last few years, but he says the school is on its way toward paying down the multimillion-dollar debt. There are plans for renovation, for library improvement, for all sorts of new systems to benefit campus life. ORU, he says, is a place of strength. A place of renewal. A place where one can study any academic discipline with the confidence that comes from knowing one's instructors have been taught by the Spirit of God.

A guest minister stands up and says he wants to pray for us all, that God will help us to make a good decision, that He will bless our steps no matter what school we choose to attend, that His favor will be upon our lives. We bow our heads and close our eyes. The pianist plays mildly as the minister begins to pray. He prays along his promised lines for several minutes and then is silent. Quiet voices can be heard praying all around, in tongues and in English, and the piano continues to gently hum. Then the minister looks out over the audience and announces that God is doing something miraculous.

"The Spirit of God is here," he says, "and He is doing a miracle in someone's body. The Lord wants to bring healing into some of you tonight. Thank you, God. Yes, Lord. Hallelujah." His voice is calm and deep, like he's getting a good massage. "The Spirit of God is moving, I believe, yes, that's it, in someone's back tonight. One of you, maybe more, at least one of you—yes, Lord—right now, hallelujah— is receiving freedom from chronic back pain. Maybe you have had it for years, maybe it is more recent, maybe you've been to doctors and chiropractors but nothing has helped. But God is delivering you of the pain right now in Jesus' name. Just receive. Receive your healing in Jesus' name."

This is new to me. It is in context with similar charismatic experiences—physical healing, God delivering secret information to the minister—but it is in a manner I've not yet seen. I look around and notice that I am the only one looking around. I bow my head again. People continue to pray, a little louder now, thanking God for delivering whomever He is delivering.

"If you just received healing in your back," he says, "or maybe you are only beginning to receive it, raise your hand or stand up.

Acknowledge the healing you have received in Jesus' name. Let's see who God is healing in this place tonight."

No one stands up. Heads bowed, eyes closed.

"Take your time," the minister instructs. "Just stand up so we can thank God together."

I reach behind me and rub my own lower back. I have long suffered from pain related to scoliosis, and I check to see if God has perhaps healed me. But, nothing yet. That's OK. He must have healed someone else.

Several minutes pass and no one stands up to proclaim their healing. The minister utters a gentle, "Go ahead and receive your healing, thank you Jesus" every few moments.

Silence. The muttering prayers have quieted to a hum.

"Thank you, Jesus. Glory." He's speaking silently, seemingly talking to both us and God at once. "Let's see who God has touched in this place."

Ahem.

Sniff.

Either the person who was healed is being stubborn, or else this guy misunderstood the Spirit of God. No one is standing. No one is moving a muscle except the pianist with his placid pressing of ivory.

Finally, someone in the front row stands and claims their healing. Brandon nudges me, then whispers, "Isn't he on the ministry team?" I shrug, then nod. He looks like someone we saw on the platform earlier. I can't be sure, but the gap of time from the announcement of the healing until someone stood up is enough to confuse the moment.

President Roberts stands and thanks God and everyone in the room joins in. The applause is a bit muted at first, as if everyone, even President Roberts, is wondering what we are wondering, but it soon rises to a crescendo as we convince ourselves, or become convinced, that we have just witnessed an honest-to-goodness healing. When we finish clapping and Amen-ing, the evening ends and we return to our rooms.

Brandon and I are baffled. We sit on the floor and go over it for hours. We talk and pray, talk and pray, weeding our way through the questions. What just happened? Wasn't that fishy? We are both scared of critiquing the situation. We believe God works in mysterious ways. We believe that the minister, whoever he was, is a man of God, no doubt about it. We believe that God heals people through prayer. But something about the moment of healing smells off, something that we don't want to deal with even as it infests our senses. How can something so good and pure—God's power—feel so uncertain?

Brandon and I decide, together, that we need to trust the best intentions of the minister. Maybe someone decided to save him from an awkward situation, but that doesn't mean that someone else wasn't genuinely healed and just too shy to stand up and declare it. We perform a little psychoanalysis, acknowledging that lots of these ministers have always been in environments where physical healings are part of the ordinary—if miraculous—work of God. It's force of habit for them to believe that someone is being healed whenever God's people come together. They are not trying to trick anyone, and if they have to be bailed out every now and then, that doesn't take away from the fact that God often uses them mightily. And certainly, no matter what (we hope), it cannot take away from the fact that ORU is a good training ground for Christian living (yes, yes), and that there are lots of good people here (absolutely), and even if we meet some charismatics who go a little overboard from time to time, the good will outweigh the bad. Right?

Right.

6

The Categorical Imperative(s)

It is a miracle that anyone can afford to go to Oral Roberts University. Such is the common wisdom on campus. Several students I meet during my first few days at ORU tell me some version of the story of God's miraculous, eleventh-hour provision for their matriculation. Standing in a variety of queues—dorm check-in, financial aid, choosing your major, enrollment—during the four-day new student orientation in early August, I talk with one person after another about how they didn't even plan on applying, but the application packet arrived in the mail. They filled it out in hope but knew they could never be admitted. Once granted admission, they fretted over how to come up with the multiple thousands of dollars needed for enrollment. There was no college savings, no scholarship for which they were qualified, no way of paying whatsoever. But somehow the funds were acquired. They are here because God made a way.

Some of my fellow students tell genuinely amazing stories of mysterious checks arriving in the mail; anonymous scholarship funds; and sudden, unexpected provision from wealthy family members. One of the most memorable stories is from amiable, tanned Sean, who tells me he wanted to go somewhere, anywhere but Oral Roberts University. While he was in high school, he went to a Christian youth conference two years in a row where they randomly drew a name among the two thousand students and gave the winner full tuition to ORU. Sean won *both* years, and one of those years the keynote preacher, Rappin' Lee Wilson, prophesied to him that he would "be greatly used in the ministry." All this was a sign, Sean felt, that he had little choice in the matter. God had foreordained his education.

Stories like Sean's are in abundance during the new student orientation. They bolster my faith in a God who provides for us, but they also render my own story of provision banal, regular, *human*. I applied, was accepted, received a tiny scholarship for having a good GPA at UCCS, and covered the bulk of my expenses with multiple student loans. At this rate, I will be $60,000 in debt when I graduate in three years. I am embarrassed to share this information with my peers not because of the debt, but because it does not make for a rousing story of faith. I think God wants me to be at ORU, but I also recognize that it was as easy to gain admittance as it would have been to join a bowling league, and that almost anyone with a Free Application for Financial Student Aid can pay for school. Not exactly a faith-inspiring spiritual yarn.

But I soon learn that even the students who go the normal routes—Pell Grants, Stafford loans—often explain their financial aid in terms of God's grace. Renaldo, a thick-haired, soft-spoken guy in his late twenties, tells me how just one month ago he was loafing in Honduras. He had no job, no prospects, no place to live. He was headed for poverty and despair. God swooped down to care for him in the form of a nice family from a local church. They took him in and gave him ground on which to stand. They recognized in him a deep intelligence and simple trust in God. They suggested ORU. He called, applied, flew out even before he knew if he had gained acceptance. The admissions office told him, yes, you're in, but no arrangements have been made for payment. He spent two days fretting and then filled out loan applications and received quick approval.

God provided all the way, he tells me.

I trip upon his story's ending. So much of the story is a tale of miraculous intervention. Renaldo is down and out, and these Samaritans take him in and provide a meal, a roof, and a direction. They teach him that God has a plan for his life that involves more than just getting by; he is to become part of a life-giving community. Change yourself and change the world, they tell him, and he believes it. The course of his life shifts overnight, and suddenly he is on the campus of a private university in the United States. All this makes sense; all this seems like God providing for Renaldo. But Renaldo stresses that his student loan approval is equal to God's provision. Stafford loans are machinations of God, not the machinations of man.

I have a hard time getting past this detail as he continues to talk because I realize there are two ways of saying "thank God for student loans." There is the general thankfulness that things are right with the world: "Thank God it's a nice day" and "Thank God my test went OK" and "Thank God for watermelon." General thankfulness doesn't necessarily have any theological content, which is why it often takes the more honestly secularized form of "thank goodness." But there is also specific thankfulness, the belief that the actual Judeo-Christian Creator of the Universe has through the Person of Jesus Christ and the power of the Holy Spirit made a particular mountain move out of one's particular way: "Thank God He has forgiven my sins" or "Thank God the cancer was miraculously healed; even the doctors don't know how," or, to use an older example, "Thank God the Red Sea just parted so we could cross it and get away from those chariots." Specific thankfulness attributes a specific good to a specific benefactor.

Renaldo's thankfulness is clearly specific. He believes the Holy Spirit was involved in his FAFSA. I would have expected a general, off-hand, "Thank God my student loans were approved." That would have implied the necessary ambiguity of natural causes that even someone like me—who prays without ceasing and knows about angels and demons—might want to attribute to cars warming up quickly in winter or the mail arriving on time or FAFSAs being approved.

My friend Ian is talking to Renaldo with me, and he has a similar perspective on God's provision. He filled out his FAFSA quite late in the game, Ian tells us, and his loans have not yet been approved. "They'd probably get rejected if God didn't want me here," he explains. "But all things are possible with God. I have faith that they'll be approved."

I bang my head against their logic, but I also critique my own incredulity. I wonder if I should have asked God to be more involved in my own FAFSA, or to pay for my ORU tuition without loans. Why did God not provide for me in some miraculous manner? Was I not ordained to come to ORU? Does He want me to have student loan debt? If I had believed, or waited long enough, or pursued more avenues, would He have provided free tuition? Did I rush into this decision? Am I supposed to interpret a low-interest loan as an instrument of God's miraculous provision? Am I displeasing God by not believing that the promissory note I signed was authored not by the U.S. government but by Him?

I can believe that God wants me to be here, and I can believe that He will, later, provide a good job so I can pay back my student loans. Maybe He will even help me receive scholarships during my tenure at ORU so that my loan debt will not be too severe. I thought through all this before ever walking on campus. But hearing other people explain God's provision for them leaves me bewildered. The syllogism is inescapable: God wants me to be at this school; student loans are the way I am paying for school, so they are God's way. I never thought of this, and I feel guilty both for not thinking He can be involved with things like FAFSA and for not believing that He would have come up with something better had I asked.

In the coming months, my understanding of faith will be constantly challenged as I hear my friends, professors, and pastoral figures describe the way God works in the world. I will hear things that do not quite add up, and I will force the math to fit the outcome. I will make such statements myself, statements that I question as I make them. Faith will become a categorical imperative as I learn that, for many Christians, everyday occurrences are meant to be interpreted as faith events. Faith doesn't just answer life's big questions or help us get through the hours and days; faith works in the details. Faith is a tool, like a crowbar the believer constantly uses to pry obstacles aside, or a paintbrush to alter the appearance of the world. Even life's banalities are meant to be thought of in terms of faith; the truly godly, spiritual mind looks at life this way. Faith fills bank accounts. Faith finds shoe sales. Faith locates the best parking spots. And faith certainly navigates the minute details of application, enrollment, and financial aid at ORU.

For now, I am little more than mystified by this idea of faith-as-tool. But in the coming weeks, this new appropriation of faith will become so familiar and obnoxious that all I can do is joke about it. Brandon and I and our friends will make cynical comments—if you don't get the A you were hoping for on a test it's because "you just didn't have faith for it, brother." We have faith for good food in the cafeteria, faith that the cute girl in American History will want to go on a date, faith that the Broncos will pull out the win in the fourth quarter. But the jokes are rooted in reality, and the sarcasm is our defensive, naïve response to what will increasingly be a very real theological problem.

• • •

Orientation passes slowly, like a good camping trip. And like a good camping trip, most of what we incoming students do is walk around and talk. Brandon and I visit as many dorm room floors as we can. The dorms are separated by gender, and we quickly learn there is an established identity for each dorm floor. I live on a floor called Dominion during my first semester, and will live on one called Blitz-krieg during my second. All the dorm floors have similarly Christian titles—Remnant, Youngblood, Dunamis. Some of the floors seem to have been populated randomly, while some employ a behind-the-scenes fraternal selection process. I don't much understand the difference, but it doesn't take long to understand that there are ultrahip floors, like Youngblood, and ultraspiritual floors, like Remnant, and also floors that hold the baseball or soccer teams. Either way, each floor has a distinct culture of its own, and as Brandon and I wander about we develop a sense of the social layout at ORU: the musicians, the athletes, the rich kids, the rebels, and (our favorite) the zealots.

We meet all the good Christian men and women we might ever hope to know. Everyone is passionate. Everyone is ready to bend over backward to help a brother or a sister in need. Everyone has grand stories of Christian ministry—even the seventeen-year-old freshmen have already done a lifetime of social work. They have been on mission trips to Uganda; they have fed the hungry in Ecuador; they have worked at soup kitchens every Saturday for a year. The people we meet and develop friendships with confirm my choice of school, and even as things become puzzling over the two semesters of my ORU tenure, even as the walls of uncertainty close in, many of the people at ORU will be a reliable source of comfort.

As orientation week inches toward the first day of class, everyone begins to anticipate the Honor Code Chapel, and that with slight dread. This is where President Richard Roberts will explain our conduct to us. He will explain that an ORU student does not drink, dance, smoke, engage in sexual activity, lie, cheat, or steal. I gave up all these things a year ago (um, for the most part), so I'm not sweating it. Brandon and I decide to take the high road and welcome the Honor Code as an opportunity to be held accountable to that which we have already committed. We do not plan on smoking or drinking anyway, but this will surely ensure that we do not. We would never sign our names to something and then break our agreement.

President Roberts also explains that the Oral Roberts University dress code is strategic, a thing not to be resented but embraced and appreciated. "Here at ORU, we train young people to be model Christians in the worlds of business, medicine, the arts, and education," he tells us. "We do everything with excellence because we are pursuing God's highest purpose for our lives. An ORU student stands tall. An ORU student is respectful. An ORU student goes out into the world with boldness, confidence, and sophistication. The dress code is not a strict or unnecessary rule. It is a way of preparing you to fulfill your role as exceptional, godly businessmen and women. You will wear a suit or a shirt and tie or, for the ladies, a skirt and blouse, everyday at work for the rest of your lives. So, here you're just starting early. You're being given an opportunity to think and live like a successful Christian businessman or business-woman now." His beautiful suit is a bit too beautiful for my tastes, his hair too blow-dried, but there is no denying that he has been blessed with good looks. His dress-code–appropriate trimmed and slicked hair, crisply shaven face, and beaming smile make him look every bit the refined Oklahoma gentleman he was raised to be.

President Roberts points us toward our booklets, which explain that the dress code was designed around the common fashion of the typical businessperson. For the men: short hair. No earrings. No tat-toos. No caps. Collared shirt, tucked in smartly. Tie. Clean shoes. No sandals. Mustaches are okay, but no beards or goatees. (These facial hair stipulations are a tough sell for us grunge-happy young men of the mid-1990s.) For the women: a dress or skirt and blouse. I look this over and reflect that the dress code was written some twenty-five years earlier, and perhaps the common fashions have changed. But I push the thought aside. I want to respect the au-thority God has placed over me. Wearing a tie everyday is no big deal. President Roberts is right. This will be a pain later when I go jogging in the afternoon and then have to return to my room to get dressed for supper in the cafeteria, and I will sympathize with the girls who have to wear skirts in the freezing, bitter winter weeks. But it's no big deal. Everyone looks great all the time, and we are hon-oring the people God has placed in authority over us.

The Honor Code Chapel, like every chapel or nightly meeting, involves an extended praise and worship set with the ORU worship band. Brandon and I relish these times, as worship music is for us a journey into asceticism. The students at ORU don't often praise God with all the regular, reckless abandon we are used to in the charismatic megachurch; things seem tamer now than they did dur-ing our weekend visit last spring. We are surprised at this but see it as a challenge. Are we willing to praise God exuberantly even when the people around us do not? Are we able to dance before Him without worrying about what people think? Do we dance just be-cause that's what people do at home, or do we dance because we love to celebrate God?

We dance. Sometimes, others join us. Sometimes, they do not. Either way, we dance and shout and flail our arms. We are not ashamed. We talk about this in the privacy of our dorm rooms. Worship is another one of our categorical imperatives, an action whereby we could at the same time will that it be a universal law. Worship is a spiritual prerogative we are required to fulfill. God is worthy of worship no matter what the circumstances. The Bible says that God inhabits the praises of His people, Brandon and I tell each other. If we dance before Him, He is with us. Would we do it in a Presbyterian church? We would. Would we do it if our friends and families rejected us? We would.

Invariably, people come up to us after each service. They have been blessed by our open display of praise. They are encouraged to see two men so in love with God. Exhortations come our way long after the worship services are done. People approach us on campus: "You guys are the ones who were dancing down front last night, right? I just wanted to come tell you what a blessing you were to me." We shyly agree that praise is a blessing and remind each other later that those exhortations cannot become our motivation to dance.

In the postworship glow, Brandon and I are invited to prayer groups, Bible studies, and impromptu Last Suppers. We are among the Campus Radicals. Nearly everyone at ORU (broadly speaking) is Christian, but not everyone is radical for God. We are radical, and everyone knows it, and we soon become friends with the other students who want to live at that higher level of spirituality. Gary and Danny, who live in our dormitory, are radicals too, and they'll frequently invite us for long periods of prayer in their dorm room or on the empty twelfth floor of the building. Gary brings a bottle of Welch's grape juice and a sleeve of saltine crackers. We partake of the blood and body, then use the remainder of the food for prayer snacks. We pace around the empty floor for a solid hour or more, praying that God's kingdom would come, His will be done on the campus of Oral Roberts University. Sometimes we pray until the wee hours, asking God to multiply our sleep like loaves and fishes.

We want revival to happen here. We want the students not to be able to sleep at night because they are so passionate for God. Wake them up in the middle of the night, Lord! Don't let them rest, Father, until they seek Your face! Pour Your Spirit upon this campus in power! We want God to raise up a remnant, a group of students who are especially set apart for Him. We want to be part of that remnant.

After one chapel, the four of us are walking out of the auditorium when we bump into a crowd of students. They are standing in a circle chanting, singing, clapping in rhythmic waves. I notice that everyone in the crowd is black, and I wonder if we are interrupting a race-exclusive prayer time. In the middle of the circle is Keita, the largest, baldest, and nicest person I've yet met at ORU. He is the only member of the group I know; we have already had long, serious talks about the necessity of being sold out to God. I nod at him and begin to squeeze past. But Keita glares into my eyes and points at me, then rotates his hand and curls his finger, motioning for me to join him in the middle of the circle.

Once I make my way to him, Keita lays his hands on my head and gently forces me to my knees, facing away from him. The prayer chants of the crowd lower to a driving murmur of soft humming and varieties of tongues, human and angelic. They know Keita is about to start sowing something new in prayer, and they begin to till the spiritual ground around him.

Keita's massive hands cover my head like a skull cap, his digits descending down to my nose. I peer out through his fingers, then shut my eyes tight and pray silently in my own tongue, waiting for whatever Keita and God have in mind.

"Oh Lord, we're asking You to do a new thing today," Keita begins, deep and low. ("Yes, God. Mmm-hmm, Lord," goes the encouraging reply around him.) "We're asking You to break the stronghold of racism on this campus." ("Alright, Father. Do it Lord.") "Lord, we all confess before You now that we have been unjust toward our brothers and sisters of a different color. We have not treated all the same. We have looked upon skin, upon the external, and made judgments about the internal, about the heart. Oh, we ask Your forgiveness, Lord. We repent of racism, Father." ("Yes, yes, yes, God.") "We want to be one, Lord. We want to be united, Father God. We know that Your Word says that in Christ there is no Greek nor Jew, no male nor female, and we know that there is neither white nor black, yellow nor brown nor red. We know that we are all one, Father God, and we pray that You would now BREAK!"—he shouts, and everyone raises their own tongues to a crescendo—"the spirit of racism that hovers over this campus! We say no to racism, Father God! We bind racism and loose the spirit of unity and peace! Unity and peace, Father! Bring it now in Jesus' name!"

"Hallelujahs" arise all around me. The circle is shouting and hopping, and I rise to my feet and embrace Keita. We hug hard and long, weeping, repenting of racism in each other's ear. There is a mutual understanding between us, as there often is during charismatic prayer, that the racism we are repenting of is not our own. I don't believe that Keita has prejudged me and my whiteness, and I assume he knows I haven't thought twice about the color of his skin. But we know racism exists as a category of sin, that there is residue of that sin in all our hearts, and that, moreover and most forcefully, when we repent of something in prayer we can repent for a whole group of unrepentant people. We can repent for the community and break the chains of sin. Nehemiah and Daniel both do it in the Bible, repenting of idolatry for the whole of the people of Israel. We follow their example and do it outside the chapel auditorium at ORU. We take the sins of the racists upon ourselves and crucify those sins in prayer. We repent for every racist inclination in the hearts of the people on the campus of Oral Roberts University.

Keita has sown something new, and we all spend the next hour reaping a harvest of praise and joy. More prayers like Keita's get passed around as people lay hands on one another and pray. Some of us dance to the music in our hearts. Brandon and I run the length of the hallway and leap through the air with refrains of glory. The evening crawls to a halt as several of us linger with more hugs and prayer and whispered promises to maintain friendships and be public examples of racial unity on campus.

This is the way the remnant gets things done at ORU.

• • •

As soon as you shake hands with a new acquaintance at ORU, you begin to talk about God and His calling on your life. "What are you majoring in?" means "What has God called you to do?" Students brim with confidence in their calling. The place is filled with zealots, and as I am a zealot myself I am at home, though I feel I don't know much about my own calling. Standing in line at the cafeteria one day, I meet Brian, who has known all his life that he wanted to be a pastor. Brian tells me he's majoring in New Testament, and when I ask why (stupid question), he says with the straightest face I've ever seen, "God has called me to be a pastor, and I am hungry for His Word." I'm fascinated how someone could know God has called him to anything in particular, but as I'm about to ask Brian about this, a voice behind us chimes in: "Right on, brother. We're at the right place for that." Brian and I turn and meet Abde, a sharply dressed skinny pole of a guy who shakes my hand harder than it has ever been shaken. Abde tells us he is here to study television production and learn to be a televangelist. "You can major in televangelism here?" I ask. He grins.

After you talk about callings and imply how excited you are about God, you often move toward exhortation. You compliment one another's calling or spiritual gifting or openness to the Spirit of God. You confess a sense that the person you're talking to will be greatly used by God. You commit to pray for that person and tell them you can't wait to see God work in their life.

Time permitting, you might ask the person if he or she wants to spend a few moments in prayer. Especially if you are talking after a chapel service or hanging out in a dorm room just before bed, someone might propose that you "go ahead and agree in prayer" (because Jesus said in Matthew 18:19 that if two people agree about anything, God will do it). So, you might find yourself laying hands on or feeling hands laid on with someone you met only moments before. It is not awkward because you both felt and expressed such a connection in the spirit that neither of you wanted the moment to pass before deepening that connection and encouraging one another on toward godliness, as iron sharpens iron because where two or more are gathered so there God is with them so in Jesus' name let's just let God do what He wants to do right now in Jesus' name.

After two weeks, I have prayed with so many people after shaking hands and exchanging exhortations that I feel I know half the school. And I am constantly encouraged. Everyone has told me that God will use me greatly, and I have told everyone the same thing, and we all mean it and know that it is true. ORU is not a place of insincere devotion; it is a place of extreme devotion sincerely and frequently expressed. We believe what Jesus said about the world knowing us by our love for each other, and although the world isn't really getting a chance to know us here among the jutting buildings of Oral Roberts University, we are practicing for when they do get that chance, and by then our love will be so evident and the power of the Spirit so strong among us that they will have no choice but to be saved or deny the plain truth that is right before their eyes.

The meet-and-greet-and-exhort-and-lay-hands-on-and-pray introduction is particularly long and potent with Tim, whom I meet in my first week at school. Tim is a Midwestern conflation of Jim Morrison and Ted Nugent, and our connection is immediate. I sense that he is an unusually zealous zealot, and he knows I am an unusually worshipful worshipper. He too had had a night-and-day conversion experience, but his night was darker and his day brighter. He was mired in drug abuse in southern Illinois until one night he got saved while stoned and watching a televangelist. Since then Tim has been a true diehard Jesus freak, selling all his possessions and living on faith and getting every other person he meets either saved or filled with the Holy Spirit or both. He does not brag about any of this. He is nearly ashamed of it, for he fears that we Jesus-crazy neophytes will glorify Tim and his zealousness rather than glorifying God, and he is right. It is hard not to glorify someone who does not just talk the talk but walks the walk, and walks it with such sincere abandon that we all feel we have our very own St. Francis of Assisi right here in our presence.

Tim's drug use seems to have left him permanently relaxed—serious as all hell about heaven and hell, but relaxed. He tells stories as if he is not listening to himself. He tells me about his everything-must-go possession sale. It was inspired by taking Jesus' words at face value, combining the admonition to the rich man—"Sell all your possessions and give the money to the poor"—with the admonition to His disciples on their first road trip— "Take nothing on your journey." Tim went to California, had a sell-off, and then gave the money away, leaving himself just these things: an old car with one tank of gas, one loaf of bread, one jar of peanut butter, and one change of clothes. He headed eastward with his one tank, believing that God would expand the gas or provide a fill-up. Tim drove across America, picking up hitchhikers and taking the gospel to the highways and byways. He did it all. He got all the way to Florida, he tells me, leaving out the whole middle portion of America from his story. I know there are amazing details to hear of bikers and panhandlers and the Holy Spirit falling in cheap motels in the middle of the night, but Tim is not much for details.

Tim and I connect because he can see in my eyes (and I in his) that we are deadly serious about this God thing. We are giving our lives over to the cause of the gospel, which surely means losing most of what we love and probably dying in the deep, wet jungles of South America. We say this without saying it, all in the course of our first conversation.

The night after I meet Tim, I am sitting in my dorm room reading and waiting for a phone call. There is a knock at the door. I crack it open. Tim stands there, head slightly bowed, eyes damp. I push the door open more. "Hey, brotherman," he says. "Got a minute to pray together?"

"Sure. Good to see you."

"Actually, I just want to pray for you, Patton. I feel a deep connection between us already."

He is carrying a plastic pail filled with water. A washcloth and towel hang around his neck.

"What's that?" I ask.

"I want to wash your feet, brotherman. Will you let me do that?"

As I well know, Jesus washed his disciples' feet before He was arrested. And I remember a Southern Baptist seventh grade summer camp where we washed each other's feet at the emotional closing ceremony on the last night. I have not come across foot washing otherwise, but it will soon be a normal ritual. I will do it to Brandon when I am mad at him and trying to express forgiveness. I will do it to a minister I admire to show how his teaching has changed me. Untying someone's shoes and pulling off their socks and touching their sweaty feet, washing, massaging, and drying them is something servants of Christ do to show just how deeply they want to serve.

Tonight is particularly exciting because it is unexpected and because the foot washer is Tim, the unofficial Senior Campus Radical. He weeps as he washes, and I weep with him. Then we pray for each other and the campus and the world, and we commit to serve one another in Christ for the rest of our lives.

Other than the foot washing and infrequent prayer sessions, Tim and I hardly see each other at all during my ORU tenure. When we walk past each other on campus we hug and say how much we admire and appreciate each other, and it will be true. We will not go to movies or bowling or for hikes or out to eat. We will move in similar social circles but somehow rarely bump into one another. But when we do, we will say that we are as close as friends can be. Tim will leave ORU at the end of fall semester, never to return. I will leave ORU at the end of the year, also never to return. I will stand for him at his wedding, and he at mine, but we will hardly be in touch otherwise. We will talk twice a year, on average. During those talks over the coming years, we will gather that his theology has shown some cracks and that mine has blown apart, and we are both struggling to fit the pieces back together. We will both stay committed, to our friendship and to what we have professed to believe, but the nature of our commitments will alter in ways we never would have anticipated.

By the night of the foot washing, I have already been confused by a few things at ORU—not by anything having to do with the school in particular, but with the culture at the school. There have been some hurdles to leap over, and I have begun to worry that perhaps I am not quite prepared for all I will find here. But Tim calms those worries. He reminds me why I am here. I am here to meet people like him. Not radicals, necessarily, but people like me and unlike me with whom the connection is mysterious but unmistakable.

• • •

Most of the people I meet in my first few days at ORU are lifelong charismatic Christians, born and raised in church and filled with the Holy Spirit as kids. Many tell me they come from "ay-jee" churches. When I ask Brandon what an ay-jee church is, he explains that it is a Pentecostal denomination, Assemblies of God. "Oh, AG," I say. I am surprised that something so mechanized as a denomination could arise out of the Pentecostal tradition, but then I am surprised by a lot of my findings at ORU. I thought I knew charismatic Christianity fairly well. I'm a dancer and a Prayer Warrior. I know all about spiritual gifts and praying against demonic strongholds. But ORU reveals, or inhabits, a charismatic culture that is more multifaceted than anything I experienced in Colorado.

One day I am sitting outside reading when Dwayne walks by. I met Dwayne at the dormitory check-in and have had a couple meals and prayer times with him, and already I know that he has but two levels: high and low. If he is not bouncing with excitement, he is drowning in his own solemnity. I enjoy his polarization (not least because I'm similarly polarized), and we hit it off right away. At the moment, Dwayne is bouncing with excitement.

"Hey, did you hear that they're letting students in for free tonight?"

"No. Free into what?"

He is aghast. "The Mabee Center! For the conference?"

I shrug. "I didn't know anything was going on."

"You didn't know anything was going on?" Dwayne repeats, incredulously.

"No. Why?"

"Man, Rod Parsley is going to be there! It's going to be so powerful!"

"Who?"

Dwayne is about to pop out of his collared shirt and tie.

"Rod Parsley! Brother! You don't know who Rod Parsley is?" The question is part dubiousness, part accusation.

"Can't say I do."

Dwayne's tone changes. "What kind of church are you from?"

"I dunno," I respond, defensively. "A really big one in Colorado."

"And you guys have never had Rod Parsley come speak?"

"No, Dwayne. I don't know who he is. I've never heard of him."

Dwayne returns to bouncing. "Well, he's the most anointed minister I've ever heard! A great televangelist. He's prophetic. A powerful man of God. You gotta come, brother. You gotta come!"

Later, in Brandon's dorm room, I ask him about Rod Parsley, and he thinks we had better avoid it. He's some prophet or something, Brandon tells me, and probably too charismatic for my tastes. And anyway, Parsley is going to be the key speaker for this year's Spring Revival, so we will be able to hear him then.

If the greater portion of ORU students seem to be fully initiated into charismatic culture, I also meet several other people like me for whom the ORU world is slightly foreign—welcome, but foreign—and a chance to escape their former lifestyle. In the first few days of the semester, Brandon introduces me to Jason, a blond, tanned, baby-faced guy who looks like he just walked off the beach. Jason is from Virginia, but last year he told his mom he needed to get as far away from his life as possible, and that if he didn't he'd be dead within six weeks—his experimental drug escapades had recently led to heroin, and he knew he was "well on the way to death or hell or both, man." Every sentence ends in "man," and, like Tim, Jason's glassy eyes and shaggy hair give him the appearance of never having come down from his last high.

Jason's mom sent him to Russia. He worked on a farm, and one night while he was sleeping the Holy Spirit fell on him hard. Jason tells me he was instantly delivered of drug addiction and he has "not been able to stop smiling since, man." I point out that he is not smiling now. "In my spirit, man."

Lifelong or new, these Christians express supreme confidence in God. My faith is stirred by every new person that I meet. But somewhere deep within my heart and in the back corner of my mind, I am also threatened by these interactions. I worry about the size and shape of my faith compared to theirs. Our testimonies sometimes take the form of spitting contests. Talking with Jason, I'll emphasize my own previous drug use and "how close I was to getting into the dangerous stuff." With Brian and Abde, it's all about how powerfully the Lord reveals Himself to me in His Word. In Danny and Gary's dorm room, I get tired of praying after the first couple hours, but I act like I'm just getting started.

I know the charismatic megachurch pastor would think I am being silly. He always advised us to think less about ourselves and more about others and God. He doesn't know me, but I measure myself against his opinion and pretend that he's checking into my life at ORU. But rather than relying on his words, I begin to rely on his name. At ORU, being from Colorado Springs is almost as cool as having a great testimony. When I'm threatened by the distance of people's spiritual spit, I steer the conversation toward geographic origins because I know Colorado Springs will cover a great distance on my behalf. The city, with its explosion of big evangelical ministries that began there or moved headquarters there, is the new Christian Mecca, like Grand Rapids, Michigan, and Pasadena, California, and (ahem) Tulsa, Oklahoma, before it. In addition to my charismatic megachurch, there is Compassion International and Focus on the Family and Youth with a Mission and the Navigators and—really, the list goes on and on. So, when I am afraid I don't quite have the spiritual firepower to be a full-fledged member of the ORU spitting club, I drop the name of my home town and am welcomed (to my mind, anyway) with open arms.

But sometimes, even Colorado Springs is not enough to raise me to the higher spiritual plane.

One evening, I begin talking with an older student I've seen around campus. I've seen him praying intensely in campus prayer meetings and reading his Bible on benches. I figured him for another Campus Radical, and I have been eager to speak with him. I walk up and ask him how he's doing. He is stiff at first, but soon we're agreeing together about the glory of God, the need for revival on campus, and our desire to make His presence known in the world. I think we're having another exhortation-and-prayer destined conversation, but soon I realize he has something else in mind.

"It's all about faith, you know," he says.

"No doubt, brother."

". . ." He begins to stare into my eyes.

"Faith. That's what it's all about. Right."

". . ."

His eyes are barreling at me. My response was too equivocal. I had agreed fully with my words, but obliquely with my expression, my face dropping slightly, betraying incredulity: What does he mean it's *all* about faith?

I ask him.

"What God does in our lives and in the world is a matter of our faith in Him," he says. "The reason people don't see God is that they don't have faith. These people," he says, extending his arm across the whole campus—thereby implicating, I take it, the entire student body—"don't have enough faith. That's why God doesn't work here as much as He could. If we had more faith in Jesus He'd be showing up all over the place."

I try to agree with him, but something is off. "Sure, but don't you think God is already doing great work in people's hearts here?"

". . ." More staring. The silences are antagonistic.

"I mean, I meet wonderful Christians everyday. Lots of us are interested in seeing God work. We pray about it together all the time."

"I think people's faith is lacking." Glaring. Eyes widening. "Do you see God showing up here every day? I don't think so. Do you see people being healed, lives being changed? Or do you see people always complaining? 'Why don't my studies go better?' 'Why do I keep getting the flu?' If you have faith, God will provide everything you need." The finger is wagging. "You don't need to worry about money. You don't need to worry about sickness. If you trust God, He takes care of everything."

He is downright militant. He continues, and I realize he is preaching to me.

"If you trust God," he says, taking a step toward me and still glaring into my eyes—no, past my eyes, straight through my sockets and boring holes into the back of my head—"you will never be sick. You will never have a cold. There won't be any of this, 'God, please help me to feel better.' If you understand that Jesus is Lord of your life, of your body, that He is in total control, you should never get a cold or get sick at all."

I reach into the back of my throat and find my tongue. "I don't know about that. I know lots of faithful Christians who get colds. A cold is a cold. Cancer is cancer. It doesn't mean you don't have faith."

"No. If you trust Jesus, if you realize that He is your healer, you should never be sick. How could you be sick if you believed Jesus was your healer? Those people don't have faith."

"Didn't Jesus say there'd be trouble in this world?"

"Yes, persecution will come because our faith in Him will offend the world. But that's beside the point."

I feel trapped in this conversation. He zeroes in on me further, exploring my faithlessness. Why are my studies not going better? My clothes not lasting longer? My family not enjoying riches beyond measure? It's all because of my lack of faith.

I let him preach to me for half an hour, and then I make up an excuse to leave and escape to my room. He's a total freak, I tell myself, but part of me wonders if he is right. That night, and for several nights following, I lie awake thinking about our conversation. I turn to the Bible to see if I can wash away his bad theology, and to my surprise the Bible refuses to do what I expect it to do. In Matthew 9, Jesus heals a hemorrhaging woman and tells her, "Your faith has healed you." In the next episode of the same chapter, some blind men ask for sight and Jesus asks, "Do you believe that I am able to do this?" They assure Him that they do, and as He heals them He says, "According to your faith will it be done to you." I have read these verses before and never understood the faith of the healees as being the condition upon which the Healer would do His work. But now the role of their faith screams to me from the page. Their faith activated His healing, not the other way around.

For the first time, I begin to hesitate to read the Bible for fear of what it will reveal to me.

7

The God Who Is Where?

The professor for my technical journalism class has come highly recommended. On the first day of classes, I awake earlier than necessary, shower, iron my pants and shirt (for the first and last time all semester), dress, eat breakfast, and make my way to the Learning Resources Center. I walk the long, mirrored corridor leading to the classrooms, find the appropriate room number, and enter. The lecture room is large, wider than it is long. Almost every seat is already filled, but I spot one near the middle and squeeze toward it, settling into the deep, swiveling concave plastic. Just as I de-backpack and prepare a fresh notebook and pencil, the professor comes in, casually working his way to the front of the room. A friendly sort, it seems. He pauses several times to shake hands and make nice, like a politician working a crowd, but genuine. He is short and skinny and donned with a distinguishing rich mane of gray hair, like a Troll Doll. Arriving behind the lectern, he sets down his well-used brown briefcase and offers a soft-spoken hello.

"I love the beginning of the semester," he says, smiling, his gray hair radiating about his face, which is all teeth and eyes. "So much goodwill, so much expectation." His warmth spreads over us. "The campus is filled with young, brilliant new minds and hearts who are ready to see the Spirit of God move in their lives."

Amens ripple through the classroom. I offer one too. Never expected a professor to start a class this way, but I am rather enjoying it. I feel like giving my neighbor a hug.

"Now, to begin, I never want us to go through a class session without praying together," he says. More Amens. "So let's just start the semester that way, shall we? I love praying with my students, and I think it's important for us to feed our hearts and spirits together—just as important as feeding our minds." Amens abound. He is half-preacher and half-teacher, even more so than I expected from my ORU professors. He will guide our spirits to God and our minds to journalistic know-how.

He asks for prayer requests and writes each one on the chalkboard. He takes his time doing so, dialoguing a bit with each student who makes a request. His speech is as deliberate and underwater as his walk was, as carefree as Bob Marley. Don't worry. About a thing. Every little thing. Is gonna be alright. I figure he knows what he is doing; we will get to the syllabus when we get to the syllabus. He nominates a couple of the students to lead us in prayer for some of the requests, and at last our prayer session begins. We take it long and slow. A half hour passes, then ten more minutes, before we are done. There is no hurry, I suppose. We have the entire semester to learn about technical journalism.

I do find this a little odd, though—if only because my suspicion that things might be odd has been raised. Without really knowing that I'm doing it, I have started to compile a list of Screwy Christian Stuff: certain parts of the Bible, certain interactions with other believers, certain moments in certain church services that upset my idea of a Christianity that works the way I expect it to. My first year of Christian experience at the charismatic megachurch set in motion a train of thought that ran well, that was more or less reliable, that could be expected to just keep chugging along through familiar territory. When I arrived at ORU a few weeks ago, I thought I knew what Christianity—at least charismatic Christianity—smelled like, looked like, felt like; but I am quickly discovering the extent of my own naiveté. And, as humans often do, rather than seeking to assimilate, contextualize, historicize, or otherwise understand all this recalcitrant data, I react by (depending on the day) cowering, joking, or trying to be above the fray. But mostly cowering.

For now, as my professor and classmates linger in prayer, I try to be pleased. What could be better than studying with professors who understand that if anything is worth doing it is worth bathing in prayer? But the class session is nearly over, and I'm still wondering what the course will be about.

When the final Amen is spoken, the silvered professor turns immediately to the chalkboard—*Is that the time?*—and writes down twelve journalistic terms. "These are all the important ideas in the first three chapters of your textbook," he says. "In every class, I'll be sure to point you toward the things you need to remember. There will be no secrets here. I'm not trying to trick you."

He finishes writing the terms and says he believes we have done enough for the day. "I'll pass out the syllabi next time." He advises us to read through the opening chapters of the textbook a couple of times and come to the next class ready to go over it in detail. Hmm. An auspicious beginning. I look forward to actually hearing about journalism from this guy, and in the meantime I decide to give him the benefit of the doubt. I am attending a university where the professors understand the hierarchy of human need: spiritual, then mental. This is cool. This is OK. This isn't a bad sign. Every little thing is gonna be all right.

Later that day I'm in the gym shooting baskets with a dormmate named Niels. "How's classes, Patton?" he asks.

"So far so good. Only had Technical Journalism today."

"Bet you got plenty of prayer, then."

"Yeah," I laugh. "We pretty much prayed the whole time."

"Hope you like to pray," he says. "You'll get plenty of it in there."

My heart sinks a bit. Is this what this professor is known for? Is it why the class is so full? I have never been disappointed to be around prayer, but even my one-year-old Christian mind understands that there is a time for worship and intercession and a time for technical journalism. Surely God, the spiritual chancellor of ORU, wants us to actually study as He shapes us into people who will change the world for Him.

In the next class session, prayer requests and prayer take up the entire ninety minutes. At the session after that, the course moves forward, with a short prayer session followed by an hour-long lecture.

But at the next class, the professor says that the Holy Spirit wants to do some work in us, some work that apparently has nothing to do with journalism.

The class grows accustomed to this rhythm. As the semester progresses, the professor lectures more and more, but it is not unusual for us to spend a great portion of the class period in prayer. I'm never sure if I should bring my Marvin Olasky text or my Bible. As our midterm approaches, I wonder what exactly we will be tested on. Is this some kind of brilliant theoretical approach meant to subtly train us in accessing the power of God for our journalistic endeavors? Or is it a combination of educational shoddiness and religious malpractice?

In addition to the Technical Journalism Prayer Group, I am enrolled in a College Algebra class and two courses required for all ORU students: Health Fitness I and Introduction to Humanities. The former course is much like the basic physiology classes I remember from high school, with the addition of various levels of aerobic requirements. Every ORU student is required to train all semester to run three miles and perform certain physical feats involving pushups, sit-ups, and so on. The Apostle Paul used lots of physical fitness metaphors in his epistles, and those metaphors are splashed upon the walls of ORU's Aerobic Center so we can have proper biblical motivation as we practice our three mile run: The Body is the Temple of the Holy Spirit; Run the Good Race; Run to Win the Prize; and all that. I always hated jogging during rugby practice in high school, but now I am learning the distinct pleasure of bringing the afternoon to close with a quick three miles. I rather like the idea that God wants me to keep in shape so that I can serve Him fully throughout my life.

The humanities course is my favorite. It is exhaustive—a "bird's eye view," the professor reminds us regularly, of Western civilization. Said professor is the female component of a husband-and-wife team who have been teaching the course since the beginning of said civilization. Their lectures are, if sluggish, consistently interesting and challenging. Their primary pedagogical method, however, is not to lecture but to show a series of films starring Francis Schaeffer, the quasi-godfather of modern evangelical apologetics.

A Presbyterian convert as a teenager, Schaeffer was a Christian public intellectual in the 1970s, and he was largely responsible for whatever popular intellectual engagement was happening in American evangelicalism at the time. Schaeffer was a highly regarded lecturer and author who argued (persuasively for many) for the reasonableness of Christianity via historical and cultural analysis—scanning Western cultural artifacts from Rome forward to suggest the progression toward the problem of modernity and to explain how Christianity (specifically Reformation Christianity) can provide the answer. He was, at bottom, an evangelist, as he would have been the first to tell you. He authored books such as *How Should We Then Live?* (a reading of Western cultural history that essentially blames the disorientations of existentialism on a philosophical misstep by Thomas Aquinas) and *Escape from Reason* (a tract on worldviews that summarizes the presuppositions of a Who's Who list of important thinkers and daringly dissects them to reveal their inherent illogic).

By the time I arrive at ORU in 1994, Schaeffer is long dead, but his teaching lives on not only in his books but also in a series of documentary-pedagogical films directed by his son, Franky, who put his father's oeuvre of research on celluloid in the mid-1970s. The films, which are meant to be a cinematic companion to *How Should We Then Live?* (with which they share a title), document not only the World According to Schaeffer but also the sensibilities of the 1970s and Schaeffer's idiosyncratic chic, complete with a fantastic dress-code–breaking goatee and even more fantastic knickers. Much of the class sleeps through *How Should We Then Live?* but those of us who remain awake are overjoyed. We love the Schaeffer films, applauding them for both their cultural enrichment and their fashion anachronisms. Schaeffer is infectious. He pays attention to everything, seeing the artifacts of human civilization—paintings, statues, literature, film—as always containing eternal repercussions. The whole of Western artistic and philosophical production is assessed in light of a Christian worldview. It's fascinating. Two thumbs up.

For me, the films are an introduction to a thinker who will loom large in my understanding of what it means to be a Christian. As with much else in my faith experience, Schaeffer's ideas are something I will first embrace fully, then reject absolutely, and then recover piecemeal. I dig Schaeffer initially because he immerses me into a study of social customs and philosophy that I might have avoided otherwise. So concerned about secularism and its rampant deceptions, I need a Christian doorway to walk through into an exploration of the World of Ideas. Schaeffer gives me license to achieve a kind of awakening to film, literature, and art because he offers a Christian posture, a way of study that says it is OK to investigate the world around me and see how it fits and does not fit with what I believe. I do not realize that I need this license, but I do. The secular-Christian music dichotomy has implicated nonmusical mediums too, and the limiting paradigm, though unarticulated, works the same way. With this license in my pocket, I begin to turn my attention to the non-Christian world more and more, watching movies and listening to music and reading literature always with an eye toward what the appropriate Christian response might be.

I am not very good at it. Mostly, I cower in the face of secular wisdom. Brandon and I go to see *Pulp Fiction* and scurry to find the Christian angle but come up with nothing. All we can produce is guilt for having watched something that must displease God. Rather than discussing it on the drive back to campus, we pray together for forgiveness. I pick up *The Grapes of Wrath*, which I read adoringly in a high school English class, but now it gnaws at me as it references the Bible over and over again but rejects Christian theological possibilities and pokes at the Pentecostal preacher, Casey. In my interaction with these and other media, I cannot get much past overtly moral concerns: should a Christian let his mind reflect on sinful subject matter? Should a Christian be exposed to anything that does not affirm the lordship of Jesus and promote biblical values? I see from Francis Schaeffer's work that he was reading Michel Foucault and watching Woody Allen and Federico Fellini movies and putting them to work for his overall Christian project. I can't get beyond simple guilt, but Schaeffer sits atop the Fortress of Reason like a Christian sniper, his scope trained on everything in sight, taking down enemies with precision. Hegel, Picasso, Bergman, and infinite others receive the Schaefferian rapid-fire hit and, at least within the airtight pages of his books as I understand them, don't get back up.

But I can't climb the fortress, and I'm no sharpshooter. My instinctual intellectual reflex is not to offer a rejoinder but to give the benefit of the doubt. I feel convinced by whatever I am reading or watching. Against my spiritual inclinations, I entertain the sinking suspicion that these secular stories and philosophies might be more accurate portrayals of the world than my own. At times, every other point of view—even Steinbeck's, even Tarantino's—seems more viable to me, as if they know something I don't know, as if my Christian experience of the world has been too limited and maybe I should take their way of thinking into consideration.

I think these thoughts and then pray against them. I pray without ceasing as I read books and watch movies because I feel I cannot resist the onslaught of their influence. I ask for God's guidance as the lights go down in a movie theater. I beg for insight, for some kernel of truth, for the key to unlock these misleading mysteries and expose them for what they are. I hope one day to be able to read secular culture the way Schaeffer does, but for now I fear that secular culture is reading me.

The more I study Schaeffer and try to let him teach me how to locate and debunk secular presuppositions, the more I find that there is something inherently unsettling in one of Schaeffer's own presuppositions. His square Reformation Christianity peg does not quite fit into my round charismatic Christianity hole. His working premise, which is reinforced for me and Brandon as we read and discuss *Escape from Reason*, *The God Who Is There*, *Whatever Happened to the Human Race?*, and other Schaeffer books on our own, is that Christianity is eminently reasonable because God is the Author of all Reason. Schaeffer explains that there is a step-by-step logical progression that should lead one straight to Jesus, with the inherently true, verifiable, inerrant Scriptures paving the way. Any other mode of arriving at belief in God, he says, is an irrational leap of faith, which equals existentialism, which equals despair.

According to this way of explaining things, my charismatic friends and I are all existentialist Christians, and therefore, if I understand Schaeffer, not really Christians at all. In *Escape from Reason*, he writes, "The evangelical Christian needs to be careful because some evangelicals have recently been asserting that what matters is not setting out to prove or disprove propositions; what matters is an encounter with Jesus. . . . Why should it not just as well be an encounter under the name Vishnu? Indeed, why should one not seek an experience, without the use of any such words, in a drug experience?" This blows my hair back. Schaeffer is talking about charismatics here, right? Who am I, if not the evangelical Christian needing to be careful, along with virtually every other Christian I know? My charismatic friends and I never discuss propositions. We *only* talk about encounters with Jesus. Our whole view of God is rooted in a series of encounters; the encounter *is* our proposition. I have taken the verifiability of the Scriptures for granted, and I know I could never defend that notion except by repeating it. I know the unerring power of the Scriptures by experience, but Schaeffer wants me to understand this doctrine intellectually, to know it, to embrace it with all my mind and not flinch in the face of alternative philosophies. That seems to me an impossible task.

So I can neither critique the secular world around me as a Christian should, à la Schaeffer, nor affirm my own religious beliefs reasonably as a Christian should, à la Schaeffer. He has convinced me that there is a certainty that I am supposed to achieve, an advanced, mature knowingness that is available to those who question things. Books with titles such as *The God Who Is There* stress a front-and-center confidence. But I cannot find that certainty. I believe it exists— I really do, because it must, it absolutely has to, because otherwise the whole thing falls apart, right?—but I am unable to see it. I *feel* certain of God when I pray, and especially when I worship, but now I begin to investigate that feeling, to examine its contours, to put it to the test of reason in the way I imagine Schaeffer might do.

Part of what I'm bumping up against is the irony of learning about Western civilization from a Reformed Christian framework at a charismatic university that specializes in supernatural Christian experiences. The kind of Christianity I am living is different, by at least a few degrees, from the kind of Christianity I am learning about in Introduction to Humanities. But there seems to be no space in which to explore those differences; we proceed under the assumption that Schaeffer's Christian approach is the same as our Christian approach. And indeed, Schaeffer's confidence in the verifiability of the Bible and the reasonableness of Christianity is reinforced by the prevailing wisdom among my friends and me that nothing is equivocal; there is a way of believing in God, and you should know what that way is. Certainty does exist; it exists by faith. We put up with each other's idiosyncratic worship and prayer styles and even allow different interpretations of prophecy, but we also maintain that there is just one way of perceiving the world. There is a black and there is a white, and the gray area that exists is occupied by people who are wrong, people who don't know God at all, or don't know Him the way they should.

Still, when I'm honest with myself, I know that Christianity seems more varied than it did a year ago; the experience of differing expressions of faith even within the tight boundaries of charismatic Christianity has suggested, disturbingly, just how much personal experience has to do with faith formation. I still feel desperate to know God more, to be a lover of Christ who traverses to ever deeper levels of intimacy. I think that with enough prayer and humility will come mountain-moving faith; I will see the lame walk, I will have X-ray vision of the world, I will know God as only the radical few can know Him. But now I wonder if my zeal is itself conditional. Do I want to know God in the way I want to know Him because that's how all serious Christians are supposed to want to know Him? Or do I want to know Him this way because I happen to be around a certain brand of Christianity? The potential cultural relativity of the nature of my belief in God frightens me, and some days I feel myself clutching to my comfortable extreme of belief so as to avoid swinging to the opposite, hell-bound extreme of disbelief.

These questions and their anxieties don't arrive in a neat package. They mount up. They hide behind corners. They lurk in shadows. And even as they reveal themselves and mount one on top of the other, they exist only in skeletal form. They don't get in the way of, say, worship dancing (much) or prayer or quickly formed best friendships with other zealots. And I know that the questions I'm asking are questions that other smarter better holier Christians before me have asked, and if I'm patient enough and prayerful enough, every little thing really will be all right.

But.

Ahem.

I.

Have.

A.

Way.

Of.

Well.

I.

Can't.

Quite.

Um.

Here's the thing. Here's what I do. Here's my way of getting through. Not thinking. Not seeking council. Not reading. Not being patient. But things like this:

One day I wake up feeling I have no flesh. My bare bones face the world. The chill of air is all around me. As I get out of bed and dress for class, I move in slow-mo. I walk across the campus dragging my feet. At breakfast, the food won't quite reach my mouth. In lecture, I can barely hear the professor. I make scratches on my notepad but cannot form complete thoughts. My clothes feel like paper. I am not sad. I am dead. Have I become ill? Do I have mono? My friend Mauri asks what's wrong. Nothing, I say, blankly. Are you sure? No. But let's not talk.

I know God must be doing something in me, and before lunch I decide that I know what it is. He is showing me what life would be like without His Spirit. Yes, that must be it. The more I think about it the more it makes sense. I am numb. I am devoid of feeling. This must be what it would be like if God were to take His Spirit from me. And He can do it, too. In Psalm 51 David prays, "Take not your holy spirit from me." David must have had a day like this. Maybe God reveals spiritlessness to His most radical followers to warn them against falling away from grace.

Ten, fifteen, twenty friends ask me if I am OK today. I give them all the same response. I reply with intentional blankness: "I am fine." They know, because we are the Campus Radicals, that something spiritual is happening to me, and I know they know—in fact, I am making sure they know—but I act as though I don't care if they know. This is between me and God, or should be.

It is not until later that night, when Brandon and I are chatting about the church service we attended that ended with two straight hours of spontaneous praise and worship, that I reconsider my assessment of my day. We are sitting in a stairwell in the dormitory, and I do my best to explain my day to him.

"That's strange, man," Brandon says as I finish. "What do you think? Didn't you sleep enough last night?"

I sigh. "No, Brandon, it's not that. It's God. He is showing me what life would be like without His Spirit.

Brandon doesn't flinch. I wonder if he secretly thinks I am being foolish, but I glance at his bald head and know that he probably does not. (Brandon Bic'd his head recently after he thought that God told him not to date women for a while, and then later he hinted to me that he had just wanted to have a shaved head—if anything, more girls were touching his head than ever before.) At any rate, even as I gauge Brandon's reaction I realize what I'm saying is not true. I've made the whole thing up. I do not pause, I do not tell Brandon this. I keep explaining the wonder of God's awful revelation. What a gift He has given me, to show me how dead life would be without Him. What an honor to have the Almighty God treat me this way, reveal these secret things to me. But the back of my mind screams that everything I am saying is wrong. I want to interrupt

myself, to say, "Wait. No. Brandon, this isn't right. It's a fabrication." I want to say that, but to do it would be to confess that I am
a liar, that I am an actor, that I am a zealot for show, that I am an
immature nutty little histrionic adolescent of a Christian.

•   •   •

While questions emerge, and while Brandon and I are developing a
distinct distaste for certain aspects of a culture that we naïvely
thought would be a kind of utopia, we remain in a regular state of
awe of the fact that we are attending this school—an awe that is as
much a bemused "What the heck are we doing here?" as it is a grateful "Thank God we attend ORU!" In dark nightly walks around
campus, we discuss how the odd-looking buildings are symbols of
how it feels to believe something as odd and socially unacceptable
as charismatic Christianity. It is a strange thing to want to fit in
with the world at large, to dress like everybody else, listen to the
same music, follow the same sports teams, and then, in the privacy
of our bedrooms, to speak in tongues, to not eat food for several days
at a time, to interpret the words of the Hebrew prophet Isaiah as
having to do with our own lives. It is already a strange thing, and
being ORU students makes it stranger, because however far outside
the mainstream we are by virtue of being radical Christians, we are
further outside by virtue of allowing ourselves to be annexed onto
this campus, with these people, living and working in these buildings. We are the freaks of faith, and we are proud of it, but only in
certain company. We are happy to be in the presence of other seriously committed Christians, but we know we'll bear the mark of
ORU the rest of our lives, and at times that will make us stand out
in ways we'd rather not. Not far from the confines of this kind of
Christianity, there will be people who find it mighty odd that our
bachelor's degrees have a televangelist's name stamped on them.
Perhaps those degrees will stay tucked away in our filing cabinets.

At the same time, we know that the same campus grounds we
are walking have also been walked by men and women who are

changing the world in tangible ways. There are Christian communities all over the planet that are a direct result of Oral Roberts and his university. Villages in sub-Saharan Africa have food, water, and medicine because missionary students from ORU set up camp there. Orphans in Vietnam are learning to read and write because a husband-and-wife team from ORU raised funding for a chain of schools. Brandon and I have heard these and dozens of other stories in chapel, dorm conversations, and classrooms, and they have made us feel grafted onto a life-giving legacy. Good men and women of God, Mother Teresa–like people, have been trained on these very grounds to go make the world a better place. ORU is blessing the world, and we want to be part of that blessing.

Brandon and I remind each other of this when we begin to focus too much on the Screwy Christian Stuff. Since that night in the Baby Mabee, we've known that one particular challenge of our schooling at ORU will be to develop resistance to the aspects of charismatic Christianity that could turn us into cynics. What we haven't known is that those aspects will be so regular, or that our resistance will wear thin so easily. We do a good job of encouraging one another for a while, but it's easier to complain than to redeem. As the list of Screwy Stuff grows, our resistance to it wears progressively thin.

• • •

Maybe because you are so fully convinced early on. Maybe because you embrace everything so completely. Maybe because there is no periphery, just forward forward march. Maybe because that's the way you begin, when you get off course, when the light changes and you perceive things a little differently, it's hard to take careful account. It's hard to stop, to survey, to evaluate. If your faith is swallowed whole, then it also has to be choked back down when it doesn't sit well, forced past the tongue down the throat and into the pit of your stomach where it will sour and churn and want to come up but you keep forcing it down. You don't want to lose it. If you throw up your undigested faith, everyone around you will see it and smell it and know you for what you are: a faker, a zealot-turned-skeptic, a Doubting Thomas, a cynic, a sinner.

The Question gives rise to the Suspicion gives rise to the Critique gives rise to the Cynicism. The seed of Doubt gets planted in the new and fertile soil and germinates and grows into the biggest plant in the garden and if not carefully tended it can choke all the tender stalks, both good and bad.

No matter how much you fight off the Critique it won't leave you alone. The Critique becomes the glasses you wear during each church service, the UN translator in your ear. You notice things you've not noticed before. There sure is a lot of finery in this room. Should not the money spent on these plush pews have been spent on the poor? The gold banners hanging from the ceiling, the pink-and-yellow "Jesus is Lord" sign: how gaudy. How could I ever bring non-Christians here? They'd be disgusted at our lack of taste. The pastor's hair is slicked back like one of the Jets in *West Side Story*. His suit is too nice; it is wearing him. Is that smile plastered on? Does he mean anything he is saying? Has he ever had a unique thought in his life?

The Critique won't let you enjoy the praise and worship songs as you used to. You analyze their meaning. "I can feel You, flowing through me. Holy Spirit, come and fill me up." This song is about us, not about God. Why are we singing about ourselves? How individualistic. How typical. "Everyone get on the Praise Train!" Does this mean anything at all? You doubt it. We are not worshipping. Even those of us who think they are, are not. They are fooling themselves. They are working up emotions that are not real to express devotion to a God they don't even understand, a God they've never questioned, a God they've believed in as simply as breathing in and out. Have they ever read Exodus past the parting of the Red Sea? Gotten to the hard stuff?

The Critique pays attention to everyone around you. Everyone dancing, raising their hands, closing their eyes, and singing with oh-so-much sincerity. What do they know? Why do they believe? Is it just because they were raised to believe? Is there anything essential in their faith, or are they saved by association? They are all so confident that their God is the One True God. Do you want to be around such smugness?

The Critique turns inward. Why all these questions? Oh, you of little faith. You have had amazing experiences with God. You know He is real. How dare you doubt Him. How dare you doubt His people. Your lack of understanding is your own fault.

Oh, you of little faith.

8

Charismania

Near the top of the list of Screwy Stuff: Naming it and claiming it. Prayers that name what the pray-er wants, and claim what the pray-er wants. Name it and claim it, goes the imperative. If you name it and claim it, you will get it.

My mind is boggled by this formula for the first time at a dorm prayer meeting I attend. Not bothered, not bemused, but boggled, astonished into confusion. Tossed all around. It could have been, maybe should have been, a blip on the screen, a bump in the road I hop over and move on. But, no. It is a boggling.

At the beginning of the meeting someone stands up and asks for prayer requests. Hands pop up, are called upon. Requests are taken. A sister-in-law has been diagnosed with cancer. A father is falling away from the Lord. The MCAT is coming up. One person needs help paying for overdue medical bills, another for buying a new truck so he can get to work.

After the requests, people volunteer to pray for each one. The guy who needs the truck volunteers to pray for his own request, and when he does, he names it and claims it:

"Father, You know I need a new truck, so right now I just claim a Toyota 4x4, 3.4 liter, six-cylinder, extended cab . . . red with white trim. I need low payments and affordable insurance. I just claim these things in Jesus' name. Amen."

This being the first time I've heard anything like it, I look around and expect to see everyone smiling and nodding along with the joke. But all heads are bowed, all eyes closed. The prayers continue in all seriousness, from the Toyota to cancer.

I slide down into my seat, into my boggling. This, I will discover, is a strange breed of Pentecostalism, a teaching of personal empowerment that had a heyday but is in its dying gasps. But everyone seems on board with it in this moment, and that frightens me into wondering if I am supposed to be on board, too.

Also on the Screwy list: Is Jesus mean?

I am sitting in the lighting booth at the Mabee Center, running lights for a conference (it's my work study gig; nice work if you can get it). I raise the lights at one point and lower them at another, and have ninety minutes in between to fill as I please.

I please to fill these minutes by reading the Gospel According to Matthew, but I am not pleased to discover something there that I have never noticed before: Jesus sounds rude.

The Jesus I know, the Jesus I love, is uniformly kind, caring, sacrificial, wise, supernaturally powerful. I've read the gospels regularly for over a year now and have found this Jesus reliably present. But now, for some reason, as I turn the crinkling, red-and-black inked pages in the lighting booth, a new, sterner Jesus suddenly and forcefully comes into view. A Jesus who is unhelpful. Intentionally confusing. Rude.

When Jesus saw the crowd around Him, He gave orders to cross to the other side of the lake. Then a teacher of the law came to Him and said, "Teacher, I will follow you wherever you go." Jesus replied, "Foxes have holes and birds of the air have nests, but the Son of Man has no place to lay his head." Another disciple said to Him, "Lord, first let me go and bury my father." But Jesus told him, "Follow me, and let the dead bury their own dead" (Matthew 8:18–22).

This is not the Jesus I know, not the Great Lover, the Provider of My Every Need. My Jesus is desperate to save souls. He is desirous of helping people receive His love. He is passionate for everybody, and He is so glad when we acknowledge that passion and dwell in it. He is happy when we are happy. But is the Jesus in these passages that same figure?

I am fine with Jesus being critical of His criticizers. He is hard on the Pharisees and Sadducees because they are legalists who want to control people. I cheer Jesus on as He chastises them and uses their own Scriptures against them. I even understand why He pledges to bring not peace but a sword to the earth. He says He has come to turn family members against one another, that households will be torn apart because of Him. I can appreciate this because I have seen it happen—friends who accept Jesus against their parents' agnostic will, and such.

But Jesus' harsh criticisms also reach into places I do not expect. After one parable, Jesus' friend Peter asks for an explanation. "Are you still so dull?" Jesus snaps. Worse, Jesus appears to dishonor His own family. Once when someone tells Jesus that His mother and brothers are standing outside and waiting to see Him, Jesus replies, "Who is my mother, and who are my brothers?" He suggests that His true family is "whoever does the will of my Father in heaven" (Matthew 12:46–50). I see His point, but does He have to ignore His mom? And how does this fit with my understanding of a God who wants everyone to be a part of a loving family, a God who focuses on the family and wants us to do the same?

Turning more crinkly pages, I read—as if for the first time—the story of Jesus calling a Canaanite woman a dog. She cries out to Him to deliver her daughter of demonic possession. "Jesus did not answer a word," says Matthew (15:23). The Great Lover ignores her cries. The woman doesn't let up, and finally, Jesus' disciples beg Him to do something to shut her up. "Send her away," they plead. "She keeps crying after us." Jesus will have none of it. Why? Because the woman isn't a Jew. "I was sent only to the lost sheep of Israel." Even when the woman forces her way to Jesus, kneels at His feet, and cries, "Lord, help me!" Jesus is unmoved. "It is not right to take the children's bread and toss it to their dogs," He says.

No, not *says*. He mutters. He snipes. He sneers. I try to imagine the way He must have spoken to her. Could He have said it lovingly? Please oh God, show me how He must have said this lovingly. But I know He didn't. It's right there on the page, plain to see. I've read Matthew a hundred times and never noticed it, but tonight it is leaping from the page.

Fortunately, the Gentile dog is ready with a witty retort. "Yes, Lord, but even the dogs eat the crumbs that fall from their master's table."

Jesus likes this. "Woman, you have great faith! Your request is granted." Her daughter, adds Matthew, was healed that very hour.

He rewards her faith in spite of her ethnicity. Maybe it *is* all about faith, but this kind of faith, faith-as-token, faith-as-ticket, is not what I expected from my journey into faith, not what I expected from Jesus.

There's more. Jesus doesn't always appear to want people to understand His parables (Matthew 13). So far from trying desperately to help people understand that He is the Savior of their souls, Jesus obscures the truth. He predicts quick death and destruction for people who won't believe the disciples' preaching (Matthew 10). He cries out against the cities that don't repent after He performs miracles (Matthew 11).

I can make sense of some of this. Of course Jesus is mad at people who don't repent after He heals diseases right before their eyes. Of course He becomes frustrated with the silly disciples who have to be told everything ten, twenty, fifty times before they get it. But still, on the basis of everything else I've learned about Jesus from CCM and Quiet Time devotionals, the gospels are nothing short of scandalous. Jesus storms through the pages of Matthew in a way I have never seen before, and I am frightened by it. My stomach clenches. I would cry if I were not so horrified. Why has this stuff not been explained to me? I am attending a Christian university. We should be talking about this!

But maybe the problem is that my biblical vision has been veiled. Maybe I have developed cataracts of doubt. If I cannot see in the gospels the wondrous grace of God—even after I have believed in it fully and experienced it excitedly for over a year—then something must be wrong with me.

• • •

Richard Roberts is not only a university president; he is also a television personality. Not a talking head for Bill O'Reilly or a reality show contestant, but a charismatic television program host. His

"The Hour of Healing: Something Good Tonight" is seen by millions of people worldwide every week. It is a kind of Christian talk or variety show, though there is no real corollary in mainstream television. (Christian ministry programs are their own genre.) "THOH" often opens with Roberts singing a song, a laid-back, bellowing version of "Victory in Jesus" perhaps, or an original ditty such as "Say to the Mountain, 'Move!'" Roberts then generally gives an update on what is happening with his ministry, which means highlighting conferences or telling about the way the ORU students are being ministered to by the Spirit of God. The live audience provides oohs and aahs and claps like the most faithful Oprah enthusiasts. It is, for Christian programming, very watchable, compelling television.

The central ongoing feature of "THOH" is a call-in prayer request center. The request hotline number rolls across the bottom of the screen. Operators can be seen standing by happily chatting and praying for people who are phoning in. Every now and then Roberts reads prayed-for requests off index cards and shares the results of those requests. Bob in Indiana called us three weeks ago to tell us he had been diagnosed with a lymphoma, Roberts will say. We prayed for him, you may remember, and he called back in the other day to report that on his last doctor's visit they said he was free and clear. No signs of the tumor. The doctor was shocked. So, praise God for that. Susan in Florida was having blurred vision in her right eye. She received prayer on the phone earlier this week and woke up the next day with her vision restored. Thank You, Jesus.

Roberts rattles off these answers to prayer with casual confidence, an old knowingness that God does things of this sort everyday. He is thankful but never shocked. God called him to the healing ministry decades ago, and vanishing cancer and negative X-rays are part of the daily grind.

Watching "THOH," it is not hard to see why people tune in, send in prayer requests, and choose to support the Roberts ministry. He is warm, pleasant, friendly, concerned. His shtick is an old-school television persona of the Ed Sullivan kind: smile and greet the audience and get right down to the serious business of entertainment-preachingGod'sWordprayingsingingthankyoufortuningin. Roberts has no ironic detachment—which should go without saying, but still, for anyone who has watched television since David Letterman went on the air, the sincerity can be shocking. This is a polished television experience, a tightly regulated down-home entertainment. You feel as though you are enjoying a nice casual cup of coffee with Roberts as he brings you up to date on the work that God is doing. He smiles and thanks you for sharing these moments with him.

Richard Roberts is a Healing Minister. As he often explains, when God called him into ministry He called him specifically into the Healing Ministry, focusing on restoring people's bodies to health. Roberts was surprised by this call initially. Though his father had established one of the most successful Christian movements worldwide when Richard was a child, he initially wanted little to do with it, and as a college student he rebelled. Roberts the Younger wanted to leave home, leave Christian society, leave the world of Roberts the Elder far behind. He wanted to enjoy the normal pursuits of young men—drink, women—and he dabbled in vice for a time. He had a fine, bold singing voice, and his dream was to be a famous martini lounge singer. For his first year of college, Roberts chose the University of Kansas over his father's university and quickly made a name for himself singing local gigs. But he returned to Tulsa after one year and enrolled at ORU. Roberts often explains that during his brief foray into "the world," he heard the voice of God calling him home, spiritually as well as geographically, and telling him to become a full-time Christian evangelist and healing minister as his father was before him.

It would not be the last time Richard Roberts heard God's voice. In fact, one of the distinguishing characteristics of Roberts's persona is his ongoing conversation with God. His ministry style is greatly informed by his interpretation of the idea that God gives people "words of knowledge," a notion found in the passages from 1 Corinthians that I first saw on the screens at the charismatic megachurch ("To one there is given . . . the message [or "word"] of knowledge by means of the same Spirit . . ."). Words of knowledge are suggestions given by God to His people, specific hints or instructions about something that is happening or is going to happen in the world. These words—and in the charismatic Christian vernacular, *word* can function as a shorthand noun for these messages, as in, "God gave me a word this morning . . ."—most often come while one is praying, but they can come at any time. Charismatics receive words about all sorts of things: how to pray for others, what kind of counsel to offer to friends in need, what choice to make in a particular situation, whether to move to Boston or Des Moines. While at ORU, I was given good words from utter strangers that were incredibly specific (and faith-affirming), and also wacky words from friends with good intentions. I had plenty of exposure to words, especially while listening to Richard Roberts preach in chapel each week.

Physical healing is still the primary thrust of Roberts's ministry, and it is a weekly feature of "THOH" as he receives words from God about who needs healing and from what. From time to time, Roberts will look into the camera and begin to pray for healing. He will say that the Lord is telling him to pray for, say, knees. All knees. There are knees out in TV Land that have a variety of problems, and God wants Roberts to pray for them all at once. Roberts will dialogue with God about this information as he prays. God seems to be a bug in his ear, giving constant nudges about how to pray. Roberts makes quick asides to let God know he is hearing Him: "I feel the Spirit of God wants us to pray for miracles in people's knees. (Yes, Lord. OK, Lord) Let's agree in prayer that God (All right, Lord) is going to begin to minister to knees in the next few (OK, Lord. I am doing it, God) moments. Just release your faith and agree with me now that (I understand, Lord) God is about to show His healing power." Roberts expresses the utmost patience, managing to talk to both his audience—"Let's release our faith together"—and the Lord—"OK, Lord, I'll do that, God"—simultaneously.

Sometimes Richard gets a litany of healing ideas at once. As he prays, he can see with spiritual eyes God doing healing work in the bodies of various viewers, and he explains to them what is happening just as it happens. "OK, let's see, God is doing some work in someone's eye right at this minute. I don't know quite what the problem is, some sort of stigma that you've been dealing with, I don't know exactly what, but God is healing you right now. It's the left eye (Yes, Lord)—it's the left eye. I believe (Yes, God, yes) there are seven of you out there with this problem. If you'll just reach up, or look in the mirror, you'll see that it's being healed. Praise God. And also, oh, oh, someone is receiving a miracle right now in their side. You've had a (OK, Lord), a kind of dull pain in your left side, sort of a circular dull pain, right in this area, I don't know quite what the condition is, I'm just saying what the Holy Spirit is telling me, but it's being healed this very moment. Your pain is going away right now as you receive your healing from God. Hallelujah."

To those who have never heard or seen it before, watching Roberts at work can be . . . well, it can be lots of things depending on who you are, from heartening to fascinating to jaw-droppingly weird. In my year at ORU, I admired Roberts's commitment to God, to his roots, and to the transformation of his debt-ridden school (which required both tirelessness and sheer bravery), but the general effect of his ministry style on me was bewilderment. I just never knew what to make of it. I hesitated to blame him for his showmanship, for I knew that his way of thinking about God and ministry were forged onstage and backstage of a very public Pentecostalism. As the son of the premier charismatic evangelist of the twentieth century, Roberts had been experiencing and professing the move of God's Spirit on camera or live stage since he was a toddler. But my one year of involvement in charismatic Christian circles did not quite prepare me for what I experienced in listening to Roberts and preachers like him.

• • •

The required chapel services every Wednesday and Friday feature the best speakers charismatic ministry has to offer, our own little televangelist superstars that people like Dwayne are always excited to see. Between those stars and Richard Roberts himself, we have up-close and personal access to spiritual giants every week.

Though healing is a primary focus of his television program, Roberts's chapel sermons in my year at ORU are focused less on healing and more on joy. For months, in fact, the only topic he seems interested in teaching on is joy. Joy in the Lord. The Joy of the Holy Spirit. Roberts is stuck on this particular spiritual fruit—providentially stuck, as he would have it, through words of knowledge—and he spends sermon after sermon telling us all about it. He says that God keeps bringing him back to it, just will not let him get away from teaching about joy.

It all begins in a sermon Roberts delivers to the student body soon after returning from an extended trip. He explains that the Lord recently changed his life. He had lost his joy some time back, and felt awful without it, and didn't know what was wrong with him. He wondered if he had displeased God. But during this trip, God explained to Roberts that he had simply lost his joy, and now it was time to get it back, like some kind of misplaced wallet. One night, thanks to a minister who laid hands on Roberts and prayed that he would receive the Spirit of Joy, God returned his joy in dramatic fashion. He says that he laughed for several hours. Not been amused, not felt peaceful, but belly-laughed. Rolled around on the floor in hysterics. Slapped his knees and held his sides in stitches. He spent all night reveling in the joy of the Lord with other believers. They splashed in spiritual streams of joy, and now all of their lives were forever changed. Everything is different, Roberts explains. I've got my joy back! The joy of the Lord is my strength! He paces back and forth on the chapel stage in excitement, working himself up. He giggles and tosses his head back and praises God. The joy of the Lord is running through him, and oh it is so great! Thank God! Glory!

Watching Roberts do his thing, the student body reaction is as mixed as a meeting of the Senate. Some are credulous; they stand and shout along with Roberts even as he preaches, raising their hands in the air in thanksgiving that the president of the university finally got his joy back. They are the minority. Another small bunch stays seated but offers the occasional "Amen!" or clap-clap-clap. Still another minority snickers and glances all about, already thinking of jokes that will be told in dorm rooms late that night. But the bulk of us, including me, watch semistunned, waiting to see if this thing is real, and just what our University President has in mind. Will he perform a back flip? Will he do cartwheels across the stage? Will he climb the organ pipes, à la Eddie Vedder? Or will he eventually come to a standstill behind the lectern, open his Bible, and explain to us how this joy works and how to get it for ourselves?

My feelings about my charismatic culture have grown more mixed with every passing week. With every ostentatious chapel speaker, every conversation with a charismaniac, I am more dubious about the particular brand of Christian faith I have chosen to embrace, at least in its incarnation on this campus. Yet I am also suspicious of my own questions; I know that I am not too far removed from these extremes. I have committed to believe in strange things, in the Spirit of God moving in odd ways, in ways that seem foolish, almost comical. I have been living at the boundaries of human emotional experience. What Richard Roberts is saying is not categorically different from my notions of the Spirit of God leaving me entirely for one day. I don't trust what he is teaching, but I cannot let myself embrace that distrust.

Richard shares with us some Bible verses about the joy of the Lord. "You turned my wailing into dancing; you removed my sackcloth and clothed me with joy," says Psalm 30:11, and there are several other verses like it. These are indications, he explains, that God means for us to be deeply joyful about His presence in our lives. Why the long faces? Because we don't trust God. We are meant to live life to the fullest, he says, and we clearly are not living the full life, so let's fix that right now. Roberts has already been speaking for an hour, and we are creeping into our lunchtime. Afternoon classes need to begin. Roberts guesses what we are thinking and says the Spirit of God wants to do some work, and lunch and classwork can just wait or be forgotten entirely. God wants us to cancel classes and stay here and pray. He wants to share His joy with us. God is getting ready to do an amazing work in the student body of ORU, and He's getting ready to do it right now.

President Roberts feels that the Lord wants him to lay hands on every student. As he lays hands on each one of us, God will fill us with His joy. Our hearts will be fundamentally altered for the better as we experience the presence of God in a fresh way. God, Richard says, wants to perform open heart surgery, to pry open our chests and do some restorative work.

The poetry of his image gets to me. OK. I'll give it a shot. I'm ready to give him—and Him—a chance at doing some work in me.

Over the next several minutes, gobs of students form queues up and down the chapel aisles. When the aisles fill up, we pour into the hallways. We are a maze of bodies in shirts and ties and dresses and skirts, and Roberts is winding his way through us, slow but sure. I end up in the hallway. Roberts has begun to pray at the beginning of the maze near the front of the chapel, so I can't see him, but I can hear his muffled prayers working their way toward me.

"Fresh!" he is shouting. That one word, over and over. "Fresh!" Pause. "Fresh!" Pause. "Fresh!" I hear it several times before I realize that he is asking God to give students a fresh dose of joy. Oh, yes, that's what he must mean. Fresh.

I can imagine, because I have seen ministers move down prayer lines numerous times by now, that Roberts is laying his hands on the top of each student's head, praying his quick monosyllabic prayer, and moving on to the next student. "Fresh!" Pause. "Fresh!"

The prayers become varied as he moves on. "Fresh, Lord!" Pause. "Fresh, Lord!" Then: "Joy!" Pause. "Joy, Lord!" Pause. "Joy!"

Like most everyone around me, I am trying to concentrate on what is potentially about to happen. Or not. I wonder if I will fall over, under the power of the Spirit of God. I wonder if I will feel a rush of happiness. I wonder how long it will take for Roberts to get through the line—I have been standing here for thirty minutes already and Roberts still has a long way to go. But mostly, I wonder why I would believe that anything at all will happen. How is this biblical? How is it consistent with everything else I believe about the way God works? What would Francis Schaeffer think? Can I just chalk this up to charismatic weirdness and not worry about it? I cannot. I need to try to take this seriously. God works in mysterious ways. I could use a fresh dose of joy, as God only knows. But is it OK for me to believe what my instincts tell me: that Richard Roberts is operating with delusional theology at best? I want to accept the apparent truth that my university president is a freak show, but I am struck by guilt as soon as I think it. No, I need to be open. Even if Roberts is a bit goofy, the Spirit of God can still work through him. Lord, I believe You can do work in me. Lord, I am not too proud to know that I certainly need more of Your Spirit, more of Your grace. Lord, I want to be open to whatever You want to do in me today. Lord, do something in me. Please.

Please. If only to prove to me that this whole thing is not the charade it seems to be. *Please, Lord. I so don't want this to be a lie. Because if this is wrong, maybe the whole thing is wrong. Oh God, I don't want to know that what I have believed is a lie.*

As Roberts enters the hallway and my field of vision, I continue to try to pray silently but can't take my eyes off his journey through the maze. As he lays hands on people's heads, many of them fall backward. Sometimes they sink slowly as he passes by. Other times they shoot straight to the ground like they've taken a left hook. They are falling over in the Spirit, colloquially known as being "slain." The colloquialism is more violent than it intends to be. Charismatics who are slain fall over and experience a trance of unconsciousness or enlightened consciousness for several minutes, receiving revelation or emotional healing—or wondering, as I did the one time I was slain, if they have really been slain at all, or have just tried to receive whatever God was doing and then realizing that God had probably not done anything at all. Oops.

I believe that God slays people in the Spirit (it happened to King Saul and Saul/Paul in the Bible, after all) and I have friends who have had important spiritual experiences while being slain, but since my only slaying experience ended in my coming to grips with the fact that I only *tried* to be slain and did not really experience anything unusual, I am wary of it. I don't want to trick myself into it again, and I surely don't want to be tricked into it by a gung ho minister. I pray through all this as Roberts comes closer. If I experience You today, God, I want it to be real. Genuine. I don't want to make anything up.

All around me, people are experiencing the moment differently. Some are singing, some are whispering to each other, some are waiting silently with hands held out, palms turned upward in a display of willingness to receive whatever God wants to do through the university president. Unlike at Prayer Warriors back home, I am not comfortable in this varied atmosphere. At the charismatic megachurch it never felt unusual that we all were experiencing God in different ways. Our personal idiosyncrasies all somehow fit into a common whole. One of us could be dancing, another kneeling and weeping, another sitting and reading Scripture, and it was all good. It was all essentially the same. I trusted everyone's actions. Now, my trust is diminished, and I am fighting to get it back. It seems that people here at ORU subtly, without knowing it, believe very different things about God. Some people believe He provides Toyota 4x4s with the exact specifications we claim in prayer, or, rather, doesn't do anything at all until we work up the faith to make it happen. Others believe that He deals mostly in grandiose stories of love and mercy. These two Gods seem worlds apart.

I feel wrong to doubt what Roberts is doing and what my fellow students are experiencing. I rebuke the doubt. In Jesus' name. I say it aloud. Get behind me, doubt. I want whatever God has for me, even if my university president *is* a freak show.

As Roberts comes closer I cannot help but watch him work. He is sweating with the effort—forty-five minutes of moving through a dense prayer maze have exercised him. His jacket is unbuttoned and hangs open as he moves swiftly—"Fresh! Fresh! Joy, Lord!"—from student head to student head. Some receive his grip and stand, praying silently. Many others fall. Several people have volunteered themselves for the effort of catching those who fall, so no one falls hard to the ground as Saul might have. When a female student falls, the volunteers are quick to cover her legs and skirt with a small blanket. (For this I am thankful. Better not to have the temptation.)

As Roberts comes my way, I brace myself. I plant my feet, center my weight, and stiffen my neck. I want to experience the joy of the Lord. I want to be slain in the Spirit by God. But I do not want any of it to be fabricated. I will not be pushed over unless God does the pushing.

Roberts is now four people away— "Joy!"—and I am praying in tongues and (did he push that girl too hard?) trying to concentrate on my desire for God's will—"Joy, Lord!"—and (will he say "Joy" or "Fresh" for me?) God I'm sorry, I want to concentrate on You and I am not Roberts's judge I am Your—"Fresh!"—child and I want whatever You have for me even if I don't understand it—"Fresh!"—and why can't this be less—"Joy, Lord!"—confusing but Lord I open my heart to You and—"JOY!" Roberts shouts into my face as his massive hands grip my head and push harder even than I expected but I push my head right back toward his grip and before I even have time to consider that here I am getting prayed for by the son of Oral Roberts and instead of loving it and having some amazing experience of God I am resisting pushing myself you will not make me fall if I am slain I will be slain by the Creator of the Universe— before I even have time to consider, Roberts has—"Fresh!"—moved on down the line.

Nothing happens. No joy. No slaying.

I stand and pray in tongues, hands turned upward to receive from God, just in case. I don't know what to do otherwise. But I try: Thank you, Lord. For what? I guess for being with me, somehow. I trust You, even if I don't trust this. Help me, God. I'm not sure what to make of this. Is this stuff of You, or just of Oral Roberts University? Why did You want me to come here? I trust You, God. Just show me. Something. You.

I open my eyes, drop my hands, let out the breath I've been holding in. I turn my brain off and head outside.

The only thing fresh in me is a wound of confusion.

• • •

Among the student body, there are two reactions to the Richard Roberts Fresh Joy Prayer Maze: Acquiescence and Cynicism. The former is a kind of trust, and even excitement, that Richard Roberts is responding to the way God leads him. How blessed we are to have a university president who deems prayer more important than class. How wonderful to attend a school where scholastics get pushed aside the moment the Holy Spirit shows up. Matters of the heart and spirit are much more important than matters of the mind. The Acquiescers may smell the foul air of bad theology and mis-guided spiritual experiences, but they choose to ignore the bad and embrace the good. Some of my friends take this view, and I nod along with them because part of me wants this to be my view. Yes, yes. God is more important than studies. I am perfectly happy to let Him have His way with our afternoon schedule. I didn't want to go to Technical Journalism anyway.

Cynicism is more fun. A mock prayer line forms in my dorm that night. "Fresh" and "Joy" replace "Hey" and "Bye" for a couple weeks. I joke along with these people too, because another part of me wants it to be this simple, wants Roberts's antics to be just that: antics. Part of me wants him and the whole overboard charismatic impulse to be rejectable. But I fear that we are missing something in our joking. Why assume the worst of Richard Roberts, who is only doing what comes naturally to him? Like it or not, this is Christianity as we know it. If it is misguided, it needs to be changed. If it is not, then *we* need to be changed. The problem with cyni-cism, whether humorous or hopping mad, is that it is obsessed with that which it hates, and it is blinded by that obsession. Cynical eyes can no longer see the central problem but can only focus on the symptoms. Cynicism distances you from the heart of the matter. It allows you to feel superior, but not to improve things, not to redeem anything. Cynicism is not Activism. It does not form a Resistance. It is all Reaction.

At ORU, we who begin to have problems with the administra-tion or the way chapel services are run never take it upon ourselves to do much about it. We do not stage a rally or publish an underground newspaper. We do not revolt with a good old-fashioned sit-in. We talk a lot about problems, but we do no honest work to come up with a critique that, for instance, might look to the history of Christianity and use proper philosophy and sociology to offer Something Better. Instead, we joke. We become depressed. We skip chapel services and lie about it. I spend some time in this camp, and though I never give myself over to it completely, I am attracted by its charms. And I notice that even those who have breathed Pentecostal air their entire lives can choke on the fumes. Sean, the guy who arrived with two miraculous scholarships and a Rappin' Lee Wilson prophecy, seems already jaded and has been talking a lot about Buddhism.

So I feel a twinge of compunction with the Cynicism crowd, and I feel an equal and opposite twinge of intellectual and spiritual dishonesty with the Acquiescence crowd. With my closest friends—Mauri and Aaron and Jossie and Brandon—I can have long, honest conversations about it all, and though the talks are like a balm I fear that none of us have quite the critical tools we need to think about this productively—or, worse, the power to do anything about it.

I am scared to reject the whole charismatic package, but I am becoming similarly scared to embrace any of it. I sense deep problems, and although Acquiescence and Cynicism are both limiting options, I cannot think of anything more helpful. I waffle between these two positions while at ORU and for years thereafter, not comfortable with acquiescing, too skeptical of my own point of view and fearful of God to be completely cynical, and unable to find a livable medium.

Sometimes the medium finds me. Once a chapel speaker comes who breaks through all the mess, if only for a moment. His name is Rafael Green, and he is the pastor of a church in urban St. Louis. None of us have ever heard of him. He is introduced by President Roberts, and as Roberts sits down a soundtrack begins to play. Reverend Green walks toward the microphone and removes it from its stand. He is apparently going to sing us a song. Is he a singer or a preacher? He clearly thinks he is both. Brandon and I—two Campus Radicals who are becoming jaded Campus Radicals—roll our eyes at each other, and as Reverend Green sings we roll our eyes some more. His song is cheesy and forgettable, and I imagine his sermon will be the same.

But his song notwithstanding, Reverend Green is the most deliberate, articulate chapel speaker we have yet heard. Such an improvement over the song and dance numbers of the conference circuit superstars. He doesn't pace back and forth, and he is soft-spoken to a fault. His sermon is simple but substantial, all based in one phrase of one verse in Proverbs that highlights our need to have a vision for the world around us. To know God, he explains, is to know what God wants you to do, and to know what God wants you to do is to have captured His concern for people. He barely mentions the mean streets he serves in East St. Louis, but they are the context for everything he says. He is telling us to go into the rough places in the world. He is giving us a social vision. He is telling us that to serve Jesus means to serve the world, to transform our community in love.

I weep as he speaks, convicted of my self-centeredness, my exaggerated, distracting concern with the Way Things Are at ORU. Reverend Green is dealing in primary matters. He reminds me of how God's love used to make me think about other people and what they needed, how I used to know that such thinking—and doing—was the goal of my faith. I have become caught up in my own experiences of God. I have become caught up in the realization that I don't like my own culture. My distaste for my culture has distracted me; it has distanced me from the deeper things.

After the service, I walk up to Reverend Green and shake his hand and thank him. I smile at President Roberts too, grateful that he endorsed this speaker. Then I rush to the cafeteria excitedly to talk about Green's sermon with all my friends. When I arrive, they are already talking about him—what a dull speaker he was, how it was the worst chapel service ever, how they wanted to poke pencils in their eyes just to focus on something other than his droning.

My God. *My God.* This place won't give me a break. But no matter. Reverend Green has sharpened my focus, and I am going to go back to growing in Christ.

A few days later, I walk out to the edge of campus to pray. There is a hillside where no one ever goes, and I figure I can pace and pray aloud and seek God with all my heart without worrying about whether anyone is watching. I walk back and forth speaking in tongues and worshipping, just trying to forget everything and think about Him. Soon, though, I hear shouts in the distance. Turning around, looking toward the bottom of the hill, I see the man who told me I should never have another cold. He is standing straight and stiff, arms tucked into his sides, fists clenched. The only thing moving on his body is his mouth, which is opening widely as he shouts toward the horizon. I can't tell if he is shouting in tongues or making war cries. He is getting louder and louder.

I stare for several moments. My desire to pray is drained. I am standing on the same hill as *him*. I want to discredit this nutty zealot, to be nothing like him, to forget entirely about his kind. But I'm standing here, with him, out on the hillside praying, like him, as the sun goes down. He is shouting louder than I am at the moment, but God knows (surely) that I have shouted like that too. I remember the bluff in Colorado Springs where I confronted demonic schemes. I remember the twelfth floor of the dormitory where I ran and prayed. My heart sinks as I hear the man shouting, growing angrier at the devil as he gets going.

Are the two of us Christians in the same way? Is that what I am becoming? Or is it what I already am? Is anything else available?

9

The Fall(out) of the Holy Spirit

I realize that the days of doubt have come before they have fully come, because even the early days of doubt dawn with a dull, relentless glare. I do not think, *Well, I have begun to doubt what I believe, but things will likely get worse before they get better.* I do not have such foresight. I think I am already in the bad stuff. I assume I will overcome it soon; surely the trail levels off just around the bend.

But at least I realize that something has changed in me, that my mind has performed a new kind of conversion. The difference between Now, a semester and a half into the school year, and Then, when I arrived in Tulsa, is that although my faith used to be common sense—there is a God, His Son is Jesus, He loves me and moves in me, etc.—now I have to perform comic-book exploits to arrive at those same conclusions. I have to leap walls and bend rays of light and do battle with mutants. Even if I can win a minor battle and score temporary clarity, I have to work harder to achieve the old, good, warm feelings I used to associate with Christian ideas.

But things will get worse.

I will move back to Colorado, and there will be hard days there. As the summer begins, I will pray and fast for two days and break my fast not with a meal but with a joint. I will go to the mountains to pray and will strip off all my clothes and run around the woods completely naked, trying to find my innocent faith by acting it out. I will lie face down on my bedroom floor, weeping and then screaming into the carpet. I will drive my old Jeep Cherokee in the middle of the night to the plains of Eastern Colorado and consider yanking the steering wheel toward the drainage ditch as hard as I can. I will lie awake in bed wondering if I believe anything at all. I will get a dog and a bike and spend the better part of one year riding trails and screaming on top of mountain summits when no one is around. I will feed my angst with Wordsworth and Stevens and cigarettes.

I will throw my Bible against the wall, infuriated at its inscrutability. I will decide to be pragmatic about it, reading Genesis with a notebook to write down all my questions. By the time I get to the ninth chapter, the notebook will be half full, and I will give up, overwhelmed.

I will be a complete jerk. I will look down on the believers all around me, the ones for whom faith comes easy. I will decide that at least I am honest about my questions, while they choose not to think. I will poke fun at Christian music and Christian books and Christian history, piling the dirt of cynicism upon them so thick and deep that it becomes impossible to see what was good about any of those things in the first place.

I will be inconsolable.

And yet. And yet. I will not walk away entirely. I will refuse to let doubt win.

After I transfer away from ORU to a state university, I will still do the Evangelical Thing. I will lead prayer groups. I will read my Bible. I will kneel in my room in prayer. I will attend varieties of churches and respond to varieties of altar calls. I will try to reconstruct my faith with Josh McDowell and George MacDonald. I will stumble through my first dozen Eucharists.

And I will do the Too Big for My Own Christian Britches Thing. I will criticize the Campus Crusade group at my state university for being numb to the move of God's Spirit. I will lambaste my Bible study for not asking the hard questions. I will judge my roommates, who are themselves ORU expatriates, for their social drinking. I will dance in worship at my evangelical college group. I will be the only one dancing because the others' Lutheran or Baptist backgrounds have rendered worship stale. Even though I'm not sure what I believe about God, I do believe people should dance before God if they choose to worship Him. I will dance to try to reestablish my faith and to try to prove a point.

But for now, still at ORU, before all that, I only realize that I have begun to doubt. I feel different. My mind has somehow shifted. Things with God are not what they were when I arrived here. I am not comfortable. I know that some of my doubts are contingent upon my particular Christian society, but the mixture is so diluted that I can't always see the separations. Charismatic Christianity and the rest of Christendom are not like oil and water—they're more like sugar and water. And clearly, some of my questions—*How do I know the Bible is reliable? What if God is just an inevitable human construct?*—are simply the questions any believer eventually asks, questions that point not toward charismatic Christianity, but *Christianity*. Mere Christianity. Adjectiveless Christianity. But even if I were to discover a safer, more classical faith, would I want it? It's not as if I don't want to be a charismatic. I do. I want to speak in tongues and pray for healing. I want words of knowledge. I want to be a charismatic Christian who is at peace with being a charismatic Christian.

I want to start over.

• • •

Every morning when I wake up, God is in the pit of my stomach, and He is telling me to pray. Or it might be the devil. I can hardly tell the difference these days. I know God wants me to do certain things, but the devil can appear in disguise as an angel of light, so sometimes when I am told to do something good I wonder if it might be the devil and not God. I ask my peers for help with this and am told that God does not make me feel guilty; only the devil does that. God convicts; the devil accuses. So if I feel convicted, it's the Holy Spirit. But if I feel accused, then it's the devil. I must make sure that I am motivated only by conviction, and not by guilt.

Oh.

But of course the line between guilt and conviction is a hairline, and it fractures.

I wake up with the awful feeling in my stomach, the churn, the internal itch, the sickening sense that I am being asked to show devotion to a God who is already disappointed in me for needing the reminder.

I decide to just do it now. Pray now and the day will be much better. I lie back and begin quietly so as not to wake my roommate. *Good morning, God, thank You for this day.* Does God need to have me say, Good morning? In Quiet Times past, I'd always begin by wishing Him a good morning. I'd smile at my own facetiousness—there is no morning for God, you big silly—and I figured He enjoyed the greeting nonetheless. But now I say it out of habit and feel sick inside. The silliness is not fun anymore. I am not so sure God enjoys me.

Anyway, God, thank You for a good night's rest. I praise You and worship You this morning and pray that You would help me to see You today. And God, to be honest . . . well, You know that I've had a hard time seeing You lately and before I'm even thirty seconds into it my mind wanders to another strange chapel service we had yesterday and then to my Technical Journalism Prayer Hour and I think about the weird people and feel guilty for thinking about the weird people. Am I blaming them for my confusion? *I'm sorry, God. The fault is entirely mine. I don't understand the way people think about You here, but I trust that You are involved in their lives, in all of our lives. You must be. Right? You must be into what we are doing, yes? Otherwise, how could so many people sincerely seeking to know You be so dramatically misguided? We can't have been deceived, right, God?*

He wants me to pray all the time and He's upset whenever I'm not praying. He wants me to be faithful to my daily duties, but He also wants me to pray first thing in the morning. "In the morning, O Lord, you hear my voice," says the psalmist in Psalm 5:3, and as I've heard said or implied a thousand times, that is more than mere poetics of religious devotion (there is little room for poetry in our understanding of the Bible); it is an admonition to get up and seek God. "You want to know God more?" I've been asked by a thousand preachers and a thousand Bible study leaders and a thousand Christian friends in late-night Denny's conversations. "Then get up and pray."

Quiet Time used to be the favorite part of my day. I looked forward to it and did it wholeheartedly and did not have enough time to finish. I prayed like I breathed. Now I pray like I lift weights. If I do it, I feel better about myself and—it's true—I feel closer to God; I feel spiritually fit. But now my old spiritual exercises don't work. Last year, I would put on a worship tape and sing along for hours, but now my worship tapes are tired and I know them backwards and forwards. I've bought new ones, but my tastes have changed and I don't much care for the style of worship music anymore.

No one is making me feel guilty. No one is checking in on me. I do not blame those Denny's conversations or preachers, since I know they all mean well. But my shame knows no bounds. How many things is it possible to feel guilty about? Can I feel guilty about what foods I eat? I can. About what I wear? I can. About the length of my hair? I can. I feel guilty if I kiss a girl too long. I feel guilty if I watch *Seinfeld*. I feel guilty if I walk on the campus grass—staying on the sidewalks is an unenforced rule at ORU, but a rule nonetheless. All these things are potential signs that I am not perfectly holy ("For it is written, 'Be holy, because I am holy,'" says 1 Peter 1:16). I feel guilty because I have not abandoned myself completely to Christ. I am holding onto the things of this world and not the things of God.

Some mornings I am out of bed and into the shower before I think about God. Some days I make it all the way down the hall and into the bathroom and have turned on the water and let it get hot before I remember that, oh yeah, I believe in God. I need to pray. And my stomach churns. The churning is the Holy Spirit convicting me. No, it is the devil making me feel guilty. No, it is just me realizing that what used to be the plain sense of the world has become the most remote fantasy.

One Friday night I don't make plans with anyone. After supper I go up to my room and close the door and leave the light off. I am going to pray all night long. I am going to seek God. I need to deal with this thing once and for all. My experience-laden past has led me to expect an experience-laden future. For weeks, I have felt that eventually I will have an extra-powerful prayer time or altar call at which I am fixed entirely. In a merciful moment of spiritual breakthrough, the guilt will fall off and the doubt will break away and my stomach won't churn. I'll be back—back to innocence, back to clarity, back to freedom in Christ. The Bible will make sense again. I will enjoy praying with other believers again. God will fix me in a moment if only I seek Him hard enough.

As usual, I begin my prayer time by flipping through my praise-and-worship CDs. My mom recently sent me a CD from the charismatic megachurch back home, where the praise band has begun to record their own albums. It's been peacemaking to listen to—I can trust the singer's voice. I know him well enough to know he's not a weirdo. He is from the charismatic megachurch, a place where I trust that intentions are good and theology is clear and basic. No "Fresh! Joy!" Just good old-fashioned worship dancing and praying for others and teaching about the Bible. When I turn on that CD and hear those familiar sounds of praise, I remember how easy it used to be for me to believe.

But tonight maybe I'll use something else. I fear I have a tendency to rely on music too much and God too little, and tonight I need to be free of any questions, any suspicions of myself or of why things are happening the way they are happening. If I meet with God, I want it to be because He chooses to do something in me and not because I have used the balm of familiar worship music.

I decide on Keith Green. Green was one of CCM's premier singer-songwriters in the 1970s and early 1980s before he was killed in a plane crash. His music is like those emotive early Elton John ballads: big and hearty, pounding piano and quaking vocals. Keith Green wrote music for people who go into the spiritual depths, people who experience nadirs and zeniths. People like me. I play the CD softly and begin to pace back and forth. Tonight I am determined to meet with God and get this doubt thing settled for good.

I pace and pray. I kneel and worship. I focus, I "press in," as in pressing in to the holy of holies, the inner sanctum of God's presence. We can do this, spiritually speaking, if we seek Him humbly. I used to feel I could get there just about every day, but lately I've been stuck at the outer limits. Tonight, though, I'm determined to get back in. To do it, I have to leap across my chasm of unbelief, which is guarded by my wall of guilt. This will be exhausting, but I'll feel better when it's over.

As I lift my hands to God and pray, the periphery of my mind pulls me toward the corner of my desk. On that corner, at the top of a high stack of CDs, is Billy Joel's *Greatest Hits Vols. 1 and 2*. I look at the stack, knowing that the Spirit of God might be calling me to account for all that secular music. I try to push the thought out of my mind and pace back and forth in prayer. But I can't. And I wonder: is it secular music that is keeping me from knowing God? Is it the finger in the dike, and if I pull it out, will my faith flow again?

I don't really want to do this, I tell God. I mean, I'm ready to do it if you want me to. I know this is silly; it's not much of a sacrifice at all. I am totally—*totally*—willing to get rid of my secular music, God. It's not as though I'm attached to it or anything, I tell Him. It's just that I don't want to do it out of the wrong motivation. I don't want to do it because of devilish guilt. I only want to do it if You are telling me that it is keeping me from knowing You more.

Is this God or the devil? My closest friends—the unflappable Aaron, even the zealous Mauri—would tell me to get over it. This is ridiculous, they'd say. God doesn't hate your music. It's not as if you are listening to Nine Inch Nails. But I also remember the night at the beginning of the school year when Dwayne came into my room and watered the seeds of conviction (or guilt). He bounded through my door and shoved a shoebox under my nose. Several audiotapes and CDs were inside. He shook the box back and forth, rattling the media around.

"What's up, Dwayne? Whaddya need?"

"Gimme your devil music," he said. "Tonight's a night of sacrifice. We're getting rid of our music that doesn't glorify God."

"What are you talking about?"

"What is the purpose of music?" Dwayne asked me. I looked at him blankly. I didn't want to get into this. He answered his own question. "The purpose of music is to glorify God."

"Right."

"Well, do you ever listen to music that doesn't glorify God?"

"I dunno," I said, feigning ignorance. I wanted to act as though I were still a new-enough Christian to have never thought about this before. Of course I had. Since childhood. But I had never been able to up and throw it all away.

"Tonight's the night," Dwayne said. "God is calling us to account. Come on, brother. It's either all God or no God. Let's have those tapes and CDs."

I wished he would go away. I didn't want him to think I was not a committed Christian, but I also didn't want to get rid of Toad the Wet Sprocket. They were innocent enough, right? I looked over to my stack of music.

"Give it up, give it up, give it up," Dwayne chanted.

I grabbed one audiotape, *Coverdale/Page,* the album where David Coverdale of Whitesnake and Jimmy Page of Led Zeppelin hooked up to make a bunch of music that sounded just like Led Zeppelin. It was a favorite album during my senior year of high school, but it had become a guilty pleasure—in terms of taste as much as religious commitment. I threw it in the box.

"That's it, man. That's all I have for you."

Dwayne was halfway satisfied. "OK, brother. That's a start. Come to my room later. We'll be smashing these up."

Dwayne forced the issue that night, and I have not been able to forget it since. Maybe he is right. Anything that does not bring glory to God brings glory to Satan. Secular music does not glorify God, so it can only glorify Satan.

Slowly, conviction wins out. I decide that I won't be able to press in until I am rid of this devil-glorifying music collection. I put all my secular CDs in a separate stack. Counting Crows. REM. I pick up each CD and turn it over, knowing some are worse than others. These aren't exactly the spawn of Satan, I know. This isn't strict devil music. But still, garbage in, garbage out. You are what you listen to. All music glorifies something. I go through and get rid of every piece of music that I am sure does not glorify God. Stone Temple Pilots—the devil. The Doors—the devil. Toto? Pretty tame stuff, but still, nothing about it could please God. The devil.

Over the next half hour I look carefully at each title, and in the end everything that does not have a Christian industry label is pushed aside. I reduce my CD collection to Christian Contemporary Music's chart toppers. WhiteHeart. Michael W. Smith. Keith Green. And of course, Phil Keaggy and Rich Mullins. It's boring, but it's pure. I plan to take the secular CDs to the CD Warehouse to trade them, maybe for some jazz. Ain't nothing wrong with Billie Holiday, I suppose (until I read a thing or two about Billie Holiday).

Finally, I can pray. I have shoved aside the thing that was between me and God, and now that I have done it, now that I am not feeling guilty, I can proceed. I can seek Him, and I do.

Three hours later, I feel better, as I will after dozens more three-hour prayer sessions to come. I have paced back and forth and sung to God in the midst of my doubt. I have fallen to my knees in repentance of judgment and cynicism. I have flipped through the Bible and been reassured by passages that ring true. I have fought against the devil and his deceptions. I have committed to know God more—to be intellectually honest about my doubts yet determined to grow in faith.

Maybe I can make it after all. Maybe everything won't be so confusing. Maybe there are ways for me to find answers. God has pointed me toward some possibilities—namely, more prayer and reflection and sitting under the teaching of men and women older and wiser than me, whether through sermons or conversations or books. I will learn from the wisdom of those who have gone before me. I can do this. I can believe. My faith doesn't have to fall apart.

I walk to the stairwell and descend to the lobby. I figure I'll go for a walk in the night air and let all this sink in. As I am about to pass through the doorway, I see Dwayne walking toward me. I stop and stare; he seems to be stumbling. Barely holding himself up. He doesn't look like himself. He looks drunk. Dwayne? Righteous Dwayne? Sweet Dwayne? Dwayne went out on a Friday and got drunk?

I walk up to him and grab his shoulders. He gives me a sheepish grin.

"Shhelloooo, Pattshon!" He's not just drunk; he's like a drunken character in a made-for-television movie, a caricature of drunks.

"Dwayne? What's up, man? Are you all right?"

"SsshI'm fine!" His voice cracks. "I'm shhunkly dorky—ha ha—I mean dory!"

My weight is under his, holding him up. I pull us toward a chair near the front of the dorm lobby and set him into it.

"Dwayne, what did you do tonight?"

"Oh, brother, you should have been there," he says, his voice clearing a little. "This minister had the power of God. I'm telling you, the Holy Spirit was all over the place." He finds his slur. "Shol-lll overshh thish placeshhh!"

"What are you talking about?"

"We all got drunk, man. Drunk in the Spirit." He giggles.

"You got drunk in the Spirit?"

"Yeah, Patton. Shhhhit wasssh sho powerfulsh!"

Awkwardly, slurringly, Dwayne explains that he and some friends had been attending revival meetings all week at a church downtown. Tonight, Dwayne says, the Holy Spirit showed up in a major way and fell on the whole congregation. People were falling over. They were laughing. They were shouting in new prayer languages. They were getting drunk in the Holy Ghost. Dwayne drank so hard and long that some friends had to drive him back to campus. He would pick up his car tomorrow.

If, over the last few months, I have stood off to the side and held my doubt in suspension like a rubber band stretched long and thin, tonight it snaps completely in two. I don't believe a word Dwayne is saying. I'm sure he's been bamboozled. I am disgusted—not because I am convinced that God would not work this way, but because I'm convinced He hasn't done it tonight, not in Dwayne. What good can be produced of this? Dwayne is happy now, but won't he have a spiritual hangover? What will he do when the drug doesn't work next time, when his tolerance has increased to the point that he needs something even more overextended in order to feel the love of God?

I don't believe a word of it, and although the thought sickens me I don't believe that Dwayne really believes it either. I know this guy.

I know how his heart and mind work. We have prayed together, talked until all hours, studied the Bible. I know he is simply trying to serve God, to be faithful to Who he believes has created him and given him life. He's doing his best to be a Christian, but he's not experiencing anything genuine tonight at all. And deep down inside, I know he knows it.

When Dwayne finishes telling me about how marvelous the evening was and how I gotta go back with him tomorrow night, I tell him to look me in the eyes. He does, still grinning sheepishly.

"Dwayne," I say, "Be real."

"What?" he asks, still grinning.

"Just be real, Dwayne. Be real."

"Patton, brother, I am being real."

"Look, you're my friend and I love you. I'm for you. And I'm just telling you to be real. Don't experience anything you aren't experiencing."

His grin fades. He looks up at the ceiling. I walk away, leaving him slumped on the chair. I know I should stay and talk to him about this, but I'm too mad.

I don't see Dwayne for two weeks. I know that my reaction ruined his high, but I'm not sure if what I ruined was genuine or not. Though Dwayne seemed fake, though every instinct in me said that this spiritual drunkenness thing was a sham, I hold out the possibility that it could be true, and that I could be the one who is wrong. God does work, after all, in mysterious ways. Maybe being drunk in the Spirit is possible, but the form I have seen it take stinks of fabrication.

Then, one afternoon, Dwayne taps lightly on my dorm room door. "Patton, you around?" He comes in, sits down, and dives straight into what he has to say. He tells me that he has been thinking about that night, all day every day for the last two weeks. He says I was right; he was not being real, and it took him this long to come to terms with it. "Thanks for nailing me. Really. I needed it."

He looks awful, as if he hasn't eaten. His face hangs. He tells me that he has reconsidered everything, thought through all his charismatic experiences and tried to determine what was real and what was not. He believes that God has touched him in significant ways throughout his life, but also that he has made some things up. Right now, he feels there has been no greater sin in his life than that.

"It's OK, Dwayne. Lighten up a little," I say, as if I am one to talk. "We're all trying to figure these things out. All these charismatic ministers, you know, I think lots of them are just trying to do God's will. But everyone emphasizes these intense emotional experiences, and sometimes things go haywire. I've been trying for months to figure out what's real and what's not. It's tough."

Dwayne says he came by mostly to ask me to pray for him. He wants God to show him whatever God is showing me. I flinch at the idea that God is showing me anything, that any of my confusion is God-inspired. But Dwayne is sincere, and needful, and I agree to pray for him.

Dwayne's drunkenness is but a shadow of the things to come. Later that month, the annual Spring Revival begins. Classes are cancelled for a few days while a revivalist helps us drink from the wells of the Spirit. This time, I do not try to experience any of it at all. I just watch, and wonder. The final service in particular is a sight to behold. Not only are people laughing and stumbling about as Dwayne did; they are crawling around the floor. Some are slithering. Some are barking like dogs. Many are lying down, having been slain in the Spirit. But of course, it is the barkers and the laughers that hold my attention.

As I watch, I begin to weep. Not out of despair, though I am pained that I, of all people, cannot experience this aspect of God's ministry if this is indeed an aspect of God's ministry. I weep not out of conviction or guilt. I weep because I am so fed up, so exhausted with frustration. I thought I would come here and be transformed into a powerful man of God, ripe with joy and love and hope. Instead, I feel more sorrow than I ever did before I cared about God.

From my position in the back of the auditorium, I can see the whole crowd, including a man off to the side who is watching the scene much as I am. He is wheelchair-bound, and I'm not sure if he's sitting and watching because he is skeptical, or because that's all he can do. But I have seen him all over campus, even been close enough to see the gray wisp of hair above his forehead, and his reputation precedes him. I don't know what his condition is, but I know that the students call him Postie and consider him to be some kind of sage.

As I watch the fallout of the Holy Spirit, through tears, the wheelchair-bound man works his way to the forefront of my mind. I know I need to talk to him. I know he will help me sort this out. I don't know how I know, but I do.

I put it off as the hours pass. And it is *hours* that pass. People stay in Christ Chapel laughing and mourning and being slain in the Spirit forever, and I don't leave. I am stuck in the mud of my confusion. If only the veil could be pulled back. If only I could be made to see what everyone else is seeing. If only I could be made to feel it. I used to dance down there, right below the stage, convinced beyond the shadow of a doubt that God was in me and that He was alive in all of our hearts and was spreading His goodness throughout the world. But He has been made strange.

I gotta talk to Postie. I look off to the side and he is gone. I should have approached him two hours ago. I hop out of my chair and run into the hallway. I look to the right and see nothing. I move to run out the door but hear a voice behind me. Turning around, I see Postie waving goodbye to a friend. I beeline toward him.

"Excuse me, I was wondering if I could talk to you . . . ?"

"Sure, man!" he exclaims, smiling from ear to ear as if I am a long-lost friend.

I kneel before Postie's chair and let it all out. I tell him about who I was when I came here. I tell him of my faith when it was bold and new. I tell him how little by little, over the last several months, questions have arisen. I tell him how I don't want to blame anyone for my doubt, and certainly I have made my own mistakes, but I am genuinely confused by the way some people think God works. I tell him how the chapel services rub me wrong, how certain expressions of faith are off-putting, and how I never get any of these crazy spiritual manifestations that are so run-of-the-mill for others. And it's not just charismatic stuff, either. The Bible makes less sense than it did before. My understanding of who God is and how we're supposed to know Him is all blown apart. I say it all, choking back tears. I don't care that he doesn't know me from Adam. I don't know him, either, and I don't know anything about his physical condition. But I trust that he comprehends me, fully, and accepts me, unconditionally, because that is the particular leap of faith that I need to take at this moment.

Postie listens to my tirade. When I finish, he asks for my name, then says, "Patton, you are not alone." This, he says, is the number one problem of young charismatic Christians—or really, Christians of any stripe. You've accepted the broad strokes of faith, but these particularities are mystifying, and sure, parts of the Bible don't seem to add up with the rest. Some of it seems OK, and some of it is way off-base. He tells me that he is in the same boat. He has lots of questions about the Bible. He never experiences the move of God in many of the ways charismatic theology prescribes. He believes it is possible for God to work in some of these ways, but he also believes that some Christians just create their own experiences.

"But how can you distinguish, and what do you do when you know something is being fabricated?"

You can't always distinguish, he says, and there isn't always much you can do. Your job in every situation like this is to find the good, he says. Find the good. If you stay in Christian circles, charismatic or not, you will see this stuff and more. You will become more confused. But do not lose your innocence or your vigor, he says. You must do the work of faith. You must find the good. It may not be apparent, but you must work to find it, and help it along, and help others find it, and all of you together can embrace the good and reject the bad.

As Postie talks, what is happening inside the chapel seems less and less vital, less worthy of frustration. Postie prays for me and I trust his prayer. It is simple and hopeful, a prayer for faith. I leave the chapel not fixed entirely, not understanding completely, but OK with my partial understanding, contented in my brokenness.

I can see no good in any of the Spring Revival, any of the Fresh Joy Prayer Maze. All this stuff has caused my faith to hang by a very thin thread. But Postie has given me a challenge, and more important he has given me a posture, a way of approaching charismania and other Christian complexities so I'm not just standing and taking the blows. Postie has given me hope that if I work and think and stay committed to the elemental things, the clouds will part. I am thankful, and after talking with him I am more hopeful than I have been in ages.

Hopeful because I know I am not alone, and hopeful because Postie's advice implies that for some people faith is always a struggle, that it never comes easy. I can accept that now, or at least begin the process of accepting it. The days of doubt have come, and they may not go anywhere anytime soon. Even as I work through questions about charismatic experiences, the elemental things of faith— the *Who is God?* and *Did Jesus rise from the dead?* and *How can I know any of this for sure?*—will require investigation. The road ahead is long and treacherous. But I figure I can either walk the road, struggling to find truth, or I can take another trip entirely. I could move away, to Maine or California or, better, Australia. I could apologize and tell everyone, Sorry, this just hasn't worked out for me, I can't believe what you all believe, at least not in the way you believe it. I know I was dancing and yelling and speaking in tongues just a few months ago, but a new wind has blown in and nothing makes the kind of sense it did last summer. I could work at a little bookshop and form a new life. Maybe if I did that, then someday, if I talked to the right people and read the right books and so on, the truth would become clear and faith would be full and easy and I could reconvert and there'd be a great homecoming, as with the prodigal son.

Either that or I stay, and work, and struggle, because my faith used to come simply, it used to be stable and sure, all its parts in order; but now the bottom has fallen out. I don't know where it went or why, but I know it has happened. The bottom has fallen out of my faith, and I want to make sure it hasn't fallen out for good.

10

Arrested Development

When the bottom falls out you free-fall. You clutch and grab. You scan about for some place to stand, some small piece of firm ground.

When the bottom falls out, you form a new library. "Read this book," people suggest, offering C. S. Lewis or Max Lucado or the Pope. They give me *Mere Christianity* and *He Still Moves Stones* and *Crossing the Threshold of Hope*. I read the first several times and take notes. I read the last once. I cannot get past the first chapter of the second. I return to Lewis and memorize arguments for the Existence of God and the Moral Order of the Universe and the Problem of Evil. His work reorders my mind some but doesn't reapply the bottom as I want it to, as it reportedly has done for thousands of similarly inquiring evangelicals. It is not the quick, immediate fix I seek.

When the bottom falls out, hands are laid on. The accompanying prayer can be a deep and lasting solace, but it can also aggravate because the way things are prayed only adds to the questions. Why are they praying *that* way? What makes them believe God will give me peace? Should they pray that God will provide answers, or that He'll just cork the questions? Do they know what it is like when the bottom falls out? I have to have faith in their faith before I can receive their prayers for my faith.

When the bottom falls out, the Bible is an unwieldy book that is impossible to read. You read it anyway because you feel guilty if you don't. But your eyes are quick to find the inscrutable things, the Mark 4:11–12s (So parables are meant to obscure the truth, not reveal it?) and the Acts 13:48s (Only those "who had been appointed to eternal life" can believe?) and all the other biblical moments that are not consistent with your understanding of God. Even the foot-notes of your *Full Life Study Bible* don't help, don't pay attention to the plain sense of the texts. God is supposed to have revealed Himself clearly, yet how can we know Him but by the Scriptures? And what do we do when those Scriptures contradict our ideas of who He is, ideas we are taught by good Christian men and women who read the same Scriptures? So, to try to keep the bottom from falling out further, you flip to 1 John 3:19–20 (Though I might condemn myself, God is greater than me) and Psalm 139 (Nothing about me shocks God), but you overlook the psalmist's bloodthirsty senti-ments in verses 19–22 and read the Sermon on the Mount over and over. But you worry, because if you can handle only the Scriptures that say what you want to hear, you fear that you are just stroking your desire to believe, and not really believing.

When the bottom falls out, you realize that all your questions are banal. They are overasked. *Did the flood really happen? Why is the God of the Old Testament different from the God of the New Testament?* People tell you that Christians have been struggling with these ques-tions for years, and you can see that, yes, it is true. But why do the questions persist? Why do they feel so vital? If there are satisfying answers, why are you up all night; why is your faith threatened?

When the bottom falls out, you stay home Friday nights and pray. You fall on your face and scream to God for mercy, for a su-pernatural gift of faith. You ask why what used to come so simply now has to be so hard. Was it something you did? You ask for some assurance, some indication of His presence. The next day an old friend comes by and brings you a burrito and you have an enriching conversation that reawakens whatever faith lies within. You won-der if that's the answer to the prayer for assurance. It feels like it, but it isn't as permanent as you hoped.

When the bottom falls out, you are not sure how to conduct yourself in worship services. You dance because that used to please God and please you, but you have to force the dance because your feet don't hop on their own anymore. You stand and sway gently to the music, arms folded. Then you sit down and flip through the

Bible. You close your eyes and try to work up belief. You look around and envy all the people worshipping passionately, unquestioningly, and wish you were like them—faithful? confident? or just uncritical? unthoughtful? gullible?—and then *what a jerk you are for letting your thoughts go there again*.

When the bottom falls out, you fantasize about what life might be like if you had no faith. You could smoke pot without guilt. You could read whatever you want to read and see whatever you want to see. You could experiment with alternative lifestyles. You could have sex with multiple partners. You could make the most of life here on Earth, pursue fame and wealth. You could vote Democrat. You could spend all your time playing Frisbee golf.

When the bottom falls out, you want to reconstruct it however you can. You think that the best days of your life were the days you believed with full, complete, unmitigated faith. You long for those days. You want a return to them. But they are gone, and you fear they are never coming back.

• • •

The date is May 5, 1995. My CD player contains the following album: *A Liturgy, a Legacy, and a Ragamuffin Band* by Rich Mullins.

It's the only Christian CD I still enjoy, but I've worn it thin. I'm sick of Christian music, but I am even sicker of the guilt that accompanies secular music, so the CD player usually remains off. After I got rid of my secular CDs, I borrowed some new ones from my brother-in-law's fantastic collection (Why doesn't he feel guilty about owning them, I wonder?), but even though I've tried several times to enjoy Paul Simon and other seemingly harmless artists, guilt wins out. Most days I would rather go musicless than do battle against guilt, or conviction, or whatever I should call the turmoil in my gut.

The semester is over. Today is the last day of finals, and my tests are done. My plan for the day is to think and pray, to assess the last year. I plan to leave for Colorado Springs tomorrow so I can be home in time for my mother's graduation from college. She doesn't know I'm coming. She thinks, in fact, that I'm still looking for a ride home, but I've made arrangements to borrow my buddy Mauri's car. Mauri is graduating, and she will be moving to Colorado later this summer after her missions trip to India, so the arrangement suits us both. I'm looking forward to driving all night, to speeding away from Oklahoma as fast as I can.

I usually eat breakfast with dormmates, but today I want to be alone. I go to the cafeteria after I'm certain everyone will have already left. I put food on my tray and sit by a window and stare outside at the jumbling ORU buildings. For all my uncertainty of late, I have loved many things about this place, mostly the social life. I have loved the intimate time with Brandon and other friends. But what would they think if they knew the sordid details of my faith crisis? What if they knew that I was stuck in doubt, and had no idea how to move forward?

To find the way forward, first I have to find my present place, which I am hardly equipped to do. I know something is wrong with my faith, but I do not know what it is, exactly. I imagine I am in a place very much like the places of Christian skeptics before me, but I don't know how to find comfort in their company. I wish I could place their stories beside my own to find the resemblances, and take solace, but I worry that I would only be trying to assuage my doubt, and not achieving anything like true Truth.

I look out the window at the Christian students on their way to Christian classes. I know that compared to some of them I am no longer a Christian. I am not a Christian in the way I was one year ago, or even six months ago, when I knew for sure that I was a believer and was proclaiming it loud and clear for everyone to hear. I am not a Christian because I don't know how to read the Bible anymore. I am not a Christian because Christian ideas are up for grabs. I am not a Christian because prayer is work and not pleasure. I am not a Christian because so many of the Christians around me are Christians in ways that I don't understand.

I am not a Christian because Christianity is supposed to put the world into order, but for me it seems to have pulled the world apart.

I sit at the cafeteria window and try to embrace my unfaith. For the first time, I tell myself that I don't believe in Christianity, just to try it out. *But I do, God. You know I do.* None of it makes sense anymore. *Yes it does, God. I just can't see it at the moment.* I imagine what life would be like if I let everything fall away. I know I couldn't do it gingerly, casually. For me, letting go of faith would have to be as big and dramatic as coming into faith was. I'd have to talk to Kaysie and Mom and Dad and let them know. I'd have to tell Brandon. Mauri and Jossie and Aaron and all my friends would get letters. Matt and his brother John back in Colorado would get phone calls; I led them both to Christ and I'd be risking a lot by telling them about my unfaith. I'd have to engage in long talks with them, and suffer through their disappointment. How did this Campus Radical transform into an ex-Christian? I'd tell them that I was just being honest, and they'd have to accept it. I want to believe in Christianity, I'd say, but I no longer can.

In the end, I'd have to move away. I wouldn't want to be a walking symbol of Christian failure.

What do I have to lose? Friends. Family. Direction.

What do I have to gain? Honesty.

But could I be an honest unbeliever? Maybe not, because I suspect myself of having missed something. My lack of faith is my own fault, not my faith's fault. I want to continue to seek. I want to continue to pray. I want to try to believe, even if I eventually fail. If I'm going to recant, I'm going to have to fight hard first, and earn the right to reject my faith.

I turn my chair so that I can look out the window in the other direction, facing my dorm. I look up just in time to see two guys on the top floor of the dormitory hoisting a television onto a windowsill. They hold its weight back toward the inside of the room while they lean over and look to the ground. I look down, too, and see, as they do, that no one is walking by. They let the TV go. It floats through the air forever, it seems, long enough for me to think about how I heard they'd be doing this, how this was a long-planned stunt, how the television hadn't worked since Spring Break. They wanted to smash something, to watch it fall and splinter into bits of plastic and glass and wiring. It would be hilarious when it landed. It would be loud, and they would cheer, and I would laugh, because there really is something funny about throwing a huge breakable object out a window, six stories up, and watching it splatter, as long as no one gets hurt. It's especially funny here, where walking on the grass or entering the library in shorts can get you in trouble. I think all this at once as the TV falls through the air, and then it hits the ground with a PAP! followed by a screech of scattering glass. It is louder than either of the guys or I could have expected. I look around to see if anyone saw me watching, guiltily, as if my voyeurism were part of their vandalism. Out the window I can just make out the TV droppers' frightened expressions, and then they vanish. I know they are running toward their rooms and will burst inside and jump in bed, acting like they were innocently sleeping when the big crash woke them up.

As the Campus Police rush over toward the scene of the crime, I look down at my cold eggs. I feel lighter. Seeing two people having fun has broken my quagmired reflections. Maybe I won't need all day to think. Maybe I don't want anything to change. Who am I kidding? Of course I am a Christian, or want to be. I am a Christian because I have determined to do the work of being a Christian, of finding the good, of restoring faith. Maybe the problem is just one of arrested development. I have not navigated to a deeper faith, not reasoned through to discover something lasting and good. I need to find a way of progressing on to something else. I don't know what that something else is, but I know it exists. It must, because Postie found it. C. S. Lewis found it. Francis Schaeffer found it. Others have found it: a place where you can believe and not feel as though you have to jump off a cliff to do it, a place where you can achieve a kind of modified contentment in a flawed faith culture. The way forward, maybe, is just to want this, and be patient, and see what happens next.

• • •

What happens next is that I leave ORU. I leave Christian culture, as much as I know how to, and try to forge the way ahead on my own.

In spite of all the consternation and guilt, I do not plan on transferring to another university until just before I do. I do not plan on leaving, not really, not forever—not until I drive off campus after the last day of finals. A couple of friends are talking of transferring to Wheaton or elsewhere. Others—those whose parents won't pay for any school but ORU—plan to party as much as they can while away. I don't have such designs. I think I'll return home, get refreshed, and come back ready for a better year than this one, a year of more clarity than confusion, a year where I can navigate the Screwy Stuff safely. Maybe I'll start a book club.

Mauri's borrowed Jetta awaits, and I say goodbye to my friends and hop in. As I wind down the ORU driveway, I feel liberated. The further away I get, the better I feel, because I am getting further and further away from a version of myself that I had never met until a few months ago: Spiritually Confused Patton. Despairing Patton. Cynical Patton. Trying to Come Up with Answers and Failing Patton. I look forward to Colorado, where Simple Patton, Clear-Headed Patton awaits. I'll bring that Patton back to ORU next fall.

Before I get onto the turnpike, I stop at QuikTrip and buy a pack of Camel Lights, knowing I will feel guilty for smoking later, and knowing Mauri will kill me, but I don't much care at the moment. I open all the windows and crack the sunroof and smoke one after another as I race north through Oklahoma and west through Kansas. I drive as fast as possible, putting the pedal to the floor on the long flat stretches where I can tell there are no cops. I stop only when the gas needle is well below E; the Jetta needs only two tanks to cover the seven hundred miles home. For the entire drive, I praise God and smoke cigarettes. The skies open up. I pray and sing. Cruising across the pancaked Kansas interstate, I feel I have a clear connection to Him for the first time in months.

Around Salina, I realize that I don't want to return to ORU. Ever. And I realize, for the first time, that I don't have to. I am going home, and maybe I should stay there. Maybe ORU is not, after all, the place where I will become the man of God that God wants me to be. My faith seemed not only clearer, but also more urgent, when I was not at a Christian university, so maybe less Christian fellowship, not more, is the way to be a successful Christian. It's worth a shot.

Once settled in at home, I pray and fast for two days. I pray about every question and concern, from Screwy Christian Stuff to the disturbing portions of the Bible. I feel better as I pray. I am not filled with faith, exactly, but I might be well on my way. Maybe I'm discovering how to proceed, how to get through the questions, at last.

At the end of the second day of fasting, an old high school chum calls, inviting me to a party at his house. "Everyone will be there," he says. I sigh, knowing my "everyone" and his "everyone" are now worlds apart. But I agree to go, and I do, without breaking my fast. The very first thing I take into my mouth, in fact, is not food, but weed, as I sit in a garage that night and smoke away my Christian blues. It happens as an accident; it happens because I want it to. I'm too flimsy to resist. I spend the rest of the evening sitting in the front room evangelizing the prettiest girl from my high school. I was always intimidated about talking to her while we were in school, but tonight, with my brain comfortably numb and my heart stricken by conviction, I am emboldened to both flirt with her and convert her. I do my best to warn her away from the dangers of the sinful nature and offer the attractions of God's grace and love. I tell her that sin is always crouching at our door, and that God is our only hope for living lives of freedom.

"But, Patton, aren't you stoned right now?" she asks.

"Exactly," I say.

The next day, waking into a fog of regret, I do just what I did as a high school senior after partying and feeling guilty: I contact the charismatic megachurch. I get out of bed and phone the church right away—getting high while fasting is a new low that I will not recover from without deep spiritual guidance, and even then it might be too late; God might have already decided that I've gone too far. The church secretary connects me to the new youth pastor, a guy who I have heard about through the grapevine. He agrees to meet me at Chili's for lunch. He is young indeed, having graduated from ORU himself just a couple years before. His baby face and baseball cap induce immediate camaraderie, but I know I'll clench up soon if I don't blurt out everything at once. We sit and he asks me what's up.

"Well," I say, "I came home from ORU this week and decided to pray and fast for a couple days. I did and it was great but then I went to a party last night and got high and I hadn't even ended my fast yet."

He smiles. I shudder, thinking he's going to tell me I need to be baptized in the Holy Spirit. I've been there, done that, I will say. Give me something else. Before I let him speak, I pull the curtains back a bit more and reveal some details: the discouragement, the loss of faith, the confusion, the ORU oddities, the feeling that I don't belong in Christendom, and though I do still want to know God, I'm not quite sure who He is anymore.

But the youth pastor isn't going to say anything about the Holy Spirit. Instead, he tells me that he knows how it feels to hate Christian culture. He hasn't ever explored the depths of existential despair, he admits—in fact, believing in Jesus has always come pretty easy to him. It's always made sense. But look, lots of people doubt. It's a pretty common thing. You'll learn, you'll grow. And not feeling comfortable around charismatics just makes you normal, he says. As for the pot, yeah, you need to stop smoking it. But let's face it: you'll probably get high a few more times before you're done for good. You'll get stronger, and you'll screw up, and then you'll get stronger some more. Eventually, you'll get over it. It's called sanctification, and it takes a while.

Aside: this is the very thing that will happen to me over the years—the thing that happened with Postie, the thing with this youth pastor. In conversations like these, the Christian Way will appear to me as an angel of light. I will understand. I will see straight. It will look different from how any sermon or Bible study has ever presented it to me. It will look like Truth, and it will not have any of the hang-ups of entrenched evangelicalism or Pentecostalism. It might be hard, and it might be uncomfortable, and it might look like a religion for losers, but that will all be OK by me in those conversations. I will leave these moments of clarity emboldened to face my doubt.

Similar moments will come from books and articles, from particular things said in particular sermons, from songs and movies. Then, I will leave the restaurant or café or put the book down and find out whether my understanding of Christianity can hold up against my experience of the world. Often, that understanding is burned away. It's like living in a constant fugue, but not wanting to reject my faith entirely, I clutch and grab and try to make things work. Because I feel that the problem is not really Christianity, and not even Christian culture, but me. There are huge problems with Christianity as I have experienced it, of course of course of course, but there are even huger problems with me. Acknowledging this, and being part of communities that challenge the problems— personal and corporate alike—is part of what it will mean for me to continue to be a Christian.

The baseball-capped youth pastor gives me the freedom to move on, away from my postfast stoning, about which I would have worried all summer, and away from any made-up obligations to a Christian higher education. Within two weeks of talking to him, I have investigated the University of Colorado and Colorado State University and applied to the latter. I have contacted my ORU buddy Amy (the Amy of "Why do you believe in God?"), who has graduated from ORU and is already planning to move to Fort Collins with another ORU dropout, Vonda. Amy and Vonda and I decide that as long as we're all moving to Fort Collins, we might as well live together—that is, if we're leaving ORU, why not make the most of it and go in the opposite direction of the gender-specific dorms? We find a condo and sign a lease and I am enrolled at CSU before I mention any of it to my ORU friends. I figure the word will spread without my help.

A few weeks later, my friends Aaron and Jossie get married in downtown Colorado Springs. Crowds of ORU people are in town for the wedding. At the rehearsal dinner, I am in a buffet line, and ahead of me is Mauri, and ahead of her is our mutual friend Russell. Mauri and Russell are in conversation, and Russell is lost in the moment, chatting her up. He hasn't realized that I'm in the same line. I'm not exactly eavesdropping, but my ears prick up as I hear my name.

"Mauri, what's this I hear about Patton leaving ORU?"

"Yeah, he's transferring to another school," she says. "He feels like it's time for him to move on."

"Why? Money?"

"That's part of it, but I think he also feels like the English department at the school in Colorado has more to offer," she answers, dutifully.

"Hmm." He stops piling mashed potatoes on his plate and looks up toward the ceiling. "Well, I guess some people want to study literature, and some people want to know God."

Now I'm in the mood for a fight.

"What's that supposed to mean, Russ?" I pipe up.

"Oh, hey Patton," he smiles, looking down the line at me. "I'm just saying . . ."

"Studying literature and knowing God aren't mutually exclusive goals."

"No? No, you're right. Hey, I'm not judging you, brother. Just making an observation."

"Russ, I think Patton has good intentions. You haven't talked to him about this." Mauri is trying to help, and I love her for it.

"Patton, brother," Russell says, still smiling but looking me straight in the eye, not backing down, "I just wonder if you're making an abrupt decision. I know you're a seeker. I just don't see why you think you need to leave a godly university for a worldly one."

"I have great reasons, Russ. Feel free to ask me about it in private anytime." I leave the buffet line. Mashed potatoes and salad will have to suffice.

I seethe, preparing myself for more comments like that. Russell's question rings in my ears. And I wonder: *Are* being zealous for God and studying literature mutually exclusive goals? As a perplexed, emotionally burdened, overly serious ORU expatriate—fearing for my salvation, social standing, and epistemological future all at once—this is an insurmountable dilemma.

But I'm on my way to the worldly university one way or another. I'll take my chances with the literature-reading hedonists.

Russell's comment is the first and only such reaction from my ORU friends, and he is overly friendly the rest of the weekend. Everyone else is encouraging: that's fantastic; we'll miss you; you'll do well there; I've thought of transferring myself; ORU is the place for me, but it's not for everyone; and on and on. People give long, tight hugs and promises of prayer. We say goodbye without really saying goodbye, which is appropriate, because all of our journeys have just begun, and although I'll move into different versions of Christianity (and some of them will too), we'll find that the world of faith is quite small, and we'll never be too far apart.

• • •

The charismatic church youth pastor was right about pot—about both the "few more times" and the "get stronger." In Fort Collins I become a shadow version of my high school self for a few weeks and hate every moment of it. I may not know how to be a Christian, but I don't want to be anything else. I check out evangelical ministries such as Campus Crusade and Intervarsity and local church groups, but nothing seems to fit. I like them all a little but none of them a lot—and the problems, at the moment, seem much more important than whatever good may come. On Sunday mornings, I hop on my bike and ride across town to an early morning service at a Vineyard church, which suits my tastes for something charismatic, and then rush over to a Baptist church for a late morning service, which suits my tastes for something more staid. Some days I pop into Catholic Mass and sit in the back. I hope my tastes will meld, or maybe I'll discover one place complex and varied enough to satisfy my various hungers; but instead, a few months of religious taste-tests leave me nauseated. I think back to the charismatic megachurch pastor's thirty-one flavors metaphor, and how I should just pick the one I like best, but I keep thinking about how they've all been cooked up, they've all been put together by some chef's hand, none of them are essential, none of them perfect, none of them exactly true, exactly the thing I'm looking for, the thing that will satisfy and answer every contingency, every question. The one thing that will make everything make sense.

And so. That's the problem, right? That I'm looking for that thing. It's a mark of immaturity that I spend years, and years, trying to overcome.

What I do, then, is push Pause. In the early days of faith, just after worship dancing and just into long eventful Quiet Times with Rich Mullins and Phil Keaggy when I prayed for the whole world, I tried to be alone for a while, to not make friends at the charismatic megachurch, to focus on God by myself for as long as I needed. But I quickly gave that up at the offer of friendship from Brandon and others, and gave it up gladly. I needed to, at the time, because I needed other Christians to show me how to be a Christian. But now, without realizing I'm doing it, I go back to that Pause. I can't hang out with my old high school chums because the lure of their lifestyles is too strong. I can't hang out at evangelical ministries or church groups because my distaste for them is too acute—I can't appreciate their value, and I'm too self-concerned to make friends.

For a few months, I live a very quiet life. I go to class, ride my bike home, take my dog Hero on long runs, and read deep into the evenings. On the weekends Hero and I explore the foothills. We go to the river and swim, sit on the bank and watch the sunset. As the weeks go by, I read my Bible in long stretches. Sometimes I see it anew, see it for what it is. Other times my judgment is clouded and I put it down and try not to worry over it. I turn out the lights in my room and pray for hours until sleep comes. Sometimes I feel a lot better. Sometimes not. Sometimes a gem of insight from George MacDonald or G. K. Chesterton resonates deeply, and I know that

I am a believer through and through. Other times one line of one poem from William Blake, or a scene from a John Barth book, makes me slide back into despair.

Odd things happen. I meet other Christians and decide to form a prayer group at my house (it's a reflex—I'm in no position to be doing it, but it's what comes naturally). One of them is not charismatic, and I know this but I don't really *know* it, or respect it, and on the first night I begin to pray in my manner—pacing back and forth, speaking in tongues, or just saying the names of God over and over to get me into the mood—and do a nice job of freaking him out. We have debates about theological matters and both stand our ground like the silly, overly opinionated men we are. The prayer group quickly dissipates.

One of my high school friends comes to me and says he can tell I've changed, and he kind of wants to change too. When he says "change" he means that he wants to be sober—most of the time. When I hear "change" I assume he means he wants to be sober all of the time, and a zealous born-again Christian too. I do a terrible job of handling him, and within a few months we aren't talking at all.

Good things happen as well. I play a pick-up basketball game with a red-headed oddball named Peder, and our friendship is immediate. Peder is a strict Baptist fundamentalist who is experiencing theological fallout much like my own. We hike steep mountain trails and talk for six hours straight. We walk along the river all afternoon and say nothing at all.

I meet a young man who is studying to be a priest, and my understanding of Catholicism is completely reformed. He is the smartest, most devout, down-to-earth believer I've known. He, like Peder, makes me want to be a Christian.

What happens, really, in brief, is life. And life doesn't solve anything. It doesn't ruin anything, either. I make progress. I regress. I meet people who help, people who don't. I work out my faith with a good bit of fear and trembling.

The sentiments of Christian experience, in these months, are gone. The courage of intellectual argument has subsided. The easy deference to culture or tradition, the lasting and perfect comfort I might have found in the ancient wisdom of the church—that's nowhere to be found, except in the smallest of doses. But for the next little while, as I process my year of conversion and my year at ORU, I do my best to sit, and wait, for something deeper still to come. I hope something will spring up around me, or within me, to light the way. I hope to find that missing link, the key ingredient that causes life to make sense in spite of cultural oddities, scriptural conundrums, and intellectual quandaries. I hope something comes. I hope it's faith.

Epilogue
The Never-Ending Story

Can this story be over before it is Over? What does Over look like?

Is Over faith reborn? Is it renewal of early belief? Regained innocence? Is Over a maturity that sees past cultural bearings? A perspective that understands at last that God transcends everything—all the confusion and everyone's attempted answers to that confusion?

Or is Over pluralism? Can I conquer my Christian doubt by acknowledging that there may be a variety of valid religious options? Can I ever believe that Jesus is not the only way to God? Can I believe that we should not be looking for that way in the first place?

What about historical-traditional faith, the kind that has proved attractive to a documented, growing number of young evangelicals, including the ORU skateboarder Jason, who is now Eastern Orthodox ("It's all about the Eucharist, man")? Could that be my Over?

One Over that people talk a lot about is community. A story like this might end with my finding good Christian friends, people who stabilize the world, who push aside the petty things and focus on how God exists in our fellowship. It would be great to see my story be Over in that way, wouldn't it? But of course I had friends like that almost from the beginning, and have continued to know them and meet others, people who sustain and enrich me. I met such people at the charismatic megachurch and ORU, and then at conferences and parties, at bars and churches and film clubs. But community does not lead to the kind of Over I thought I needed to achieve anyway, where the questions dissipate and faith doesn't require a leap. It leads to something wonderful, but not to Over.

Maybe an intellectual paradigm shift could lead to my story of confusion being Over. "Read this book" was never exactly poor advice, especially when the advice came from a discerning reader. Indeed, lately my reading has pointed me in useful directions: paradigm-shifting histories of Christian thought, theological reformulations, stories (both fiction and nonfiction) that uproot old epistemologies and point toward new ones. Much of my reading has challenged the way I think about the Bible, fostering a new appreciation and eagerness for a text that I have had a hard time opening privately since my first year as a Christian. This has been helpful, but less like an Over than I wanted.

Over could be a genuine return home, back to the charismatic megachurch. I had such a return after college, and it was a homecoming of sorts, but it didn't produce Over the way I hoped it would. My doubt lingered even there, not because of anything I found, but because of what was already inside me. The charismatic megachurch pastor—now a trusted friend and counselor—continues to be a significant influence in my life. He serves as a living reminder that the best kind of faith is what causes you to fight for others, work for the good, and remain devoted to those to whom you've promised your love.

But there is no simple Over in terms of my faith, or my doubt. Both are still with me strongly. I still doubt. I think of it as an affliction, a disorder called Doubt. I wake to questions in the morning. Some days they hassle me all day long; other days they seem petty and foolish.

I cling to faith, too. I choose to do so.

The only honest way for this story to end is for it to come to a silent rest right in the middle. The middle is where I ended up, long after the narrative told here unfolded into new stages of life. The middle is where I remain: not rejecting completely, not embracing uncritically, but deliberating. Working on my doubt from a position of faith. As I put it to a friend recently, I believe because I believe that I have been chosen to believe. It's murky, but that's what it is. There are times when that position feels strong and bold, even unshakable. There are other times when my chasm of doubt doesn't require just a leap but rather a rope swing. And I swing away.

For years now, Christianity has been the strangest thing I can imagine, but rendered so normal in my memory and in regular evangelical experience that most of the time all I can do is poke at it, like an enormous, amorphous blob. Trying to see evangelical Christianity is like trying to see my own retina; it is that through which I perceive everything, whether I like it or not. This makes describing the range and limits of my faith, and my doubt, extremely difficult.

So, then, the middle. That's what we're left with.

There is a tale to tell of the future beyond ORU, of the too-brief years in college in Colorado, of Christian community failing and then working, and then failing again and then working better than ever. There is a tale of postcollege married life, when being a Christian took on new meaning, as did being a doubter. There is a tale to tell of great strides being made (no, *really* this time), but also of a Christmas Eve stroll where the doubts came raging back for some unknown reason. There is a tale of moving to the Northeast with my wife and forming a new life where we were constantly reminded of our middleness—we were people with evangelical pasts who were working out their evangelical futures, people who were countercultural by Northeast standards because we were very young and very married. It's not that we had a hard time fitting in; perhaps we were embraced in spite of our freakishness, though I prefer to think it was because of it. Rather, it is that we wanted to be in both Colorado and Boston and found that, surprise, we were somewhere in the middle.

There is a tale to tell of what happened next, but it doesn't lead to an Over—only to a rambling middle.

I am not alone. Lots of us are this way. Sure, you hear stories of radical young evangelicals who embrace their faith and its attendant culture—happily, comfortably so. But look to the right and the left, toward the margins, and you'll see other Christians who aren't so sure, who are put off by all that, who want to be Christians but are not certain how to negotiate a relationship with a culture that believes what they believe, but not really, and thinks how they think, but not really, and hopes for what they hope for, but not really. You'll see on those margins a bunch of people who are not actually marginalized, but middled, stuck in between. People who believe in Jesus, yes, but who have to remind themselves why. People who love God, of course, but who have trouble expressing how. People who have faith, though not as much as they'd like. But they're working on it.

I thought that faith equaled certainty, but have discovered that it's often more like certitude. It's a confidence that grows, a reliability that is strengthened over time. I thought faith would be predictable, but it is a relentless surprise. I thought my development as a Christian had been arrested, but I found that I had just arrived at this middle territory, and I realized that living in the middle can be just as useful, adventurous, and fruitful as living in the extremes. So this story has to end in the middle, because that's the only honest way to end: not perfect success, not total failure, but ambling along all the way.

Acknowledgments

Even a project as personal as a memoir happens in partnership, and there are many who helped carry this project toward completion. I must begin with my wife, Michaela, who bore the fluctuations of mood and schedule that accompany a long writing project and also contributed her editing expertise. She helped me see what worked and argued with me over what didn't—and was nearly always right. Michaela is the closest of readers, and I was grateful, as ever, to have such a sharp and ready mind at home. This book bears the marks of a harried year that packed in graduate coursework, the birth of our lovely Isabel, and a harrowing move. It also bears Michaela's wisdom and her love.

Thanks are due to my parents, Bill and Dawn Dodd, for their support through the oddities described herein, and more besides. And to my sister, Kaysie, for her stability and strength, and her husband, Mark, whose intelligence and maturity raise the bar high.

Thanks to those who encouraged the idea of this book in its infancy, especially Lisa Anderson, Lesleigh Cushing, Joshua Daniel, Miguel Garza, Nathan Humphrey, Sean Lorenz, Peter Manseau, Stephen Prothero, Steve Rabey, Jason and Laurie Redmond, and Joe and Ashley Januszewski. Thanks to those who volunteered to read and comment on the drafts: David Albertson, Jared Anderson, Rob Brendle, Peder Halseide, Cristine Hutchison, Karen and Volney James, Tim Maxson, David Skinner, and Rob Stennett. Cheryl Harris Sharman read eleventh-hour drafts before the rough-draft deadline, and her smart critiques helped shaped the final product.

Brandon Shupp read very rough drafts and then ran up his phone bills helping me think through them. He jogged my memory a time or two and corrected it at least once.

My friend and colleague Martyn Oliver was a hero in many ways. Our long exchanges in person and by e-mail were instructive and encouraging.

Peter Hawkins, my excellent doctoral advisor, was a wonderful reader and champion of the cause. He helped me adjust my academic life to make this book possible.

For the minor (and admittedly slipshod) historical notes in the Prologue and elsewhere, I am indebted to the work of many scholars, particularly David Edwin Harrell. His biography of Oral Roberts, *Oral Roberts: An American Life*, is exhaustive and smartly sympathetic, and his *All Things Are Possible* is a helpful introduction to the major figures of Pentecostalism. I also benefited greatly from the work of Randall Balmer, Susan Harding, George Marsden, Mark Noll, Grant Whacker, and others.

This project would not have happened without the efforts of Greg Johnson; thanks for taking a chance on a rookie.

My editor at Jossey-Bass, Julianna Gustafson, is a superstar.

Lastly, I wish to thank Fr. Michael O'Donnell, who set this project in motion both by initiating me into publishing and by helping me clear the fog in my head. It is to him, along with Ted Haggard and Kyle Parker, that this book is dedicated.

The Author

Patton Dodd is a doctoral candidate in religion and literature at Boston University. His writing has appeared in several publications. He has worked as a ghost writer, editor, movie reviewer, and submission director for a film festival. Patton lives in South Boston with his wife, Michaela, and their daughter, Isabel. You can learn more about him by reading this book.

A New Kind of Christian

A Tale of Two Friends
on a Spiritual Journey

BRIAN D. McLAREN

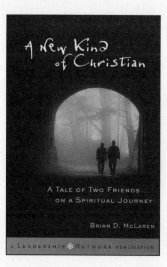

Hardcover / ISBN: 0–7879–5599–X

Winner of the Christianity Today Award of Merit for Best Christian Living, 2002

"This is a book that heightens the depths and deepens the peaks. Like all the best things in life, it is not to be entered into lightly, but reverently and in the fear of a God who is waiting for the church to stop asking WWJD, 'What would Jesus do?' and start asking WIJD, 'What is Jesus doing?'."

—Dr. Leonard Sweet, E. Stanley Jones Chair of Evangelism at Drew University, founder and president of SpiritVenture Ministries, and best-selling author

"Get ready to wake up your spirit and breath deep. McLaren's A New Kind of Christian *is a street-level, lived excursion into this present millennium—a world where ministry by control, condescension, and smug certainty gives way to incarnational faith."*

—Sally Morgenthaler, president, SJM Management Company and author of Worship Evangelism

A New Kind of Christian's conversation between a pastor and his daughter's high school science teacher reveals that wisdom for life's most pressing spiritual questions can come from the most unlikely sources. This stirring fable captures a new spirit of Christianity—where personal, daily interaction with God is more important than institutional church structures, where faith is more about a way of life than a system of belief, where being authentically good is more important than being doctrinally "right," and where one's direction is more important than one's present location. Brian D. McLaren's delightful account offers a wise and wondrous approach for revitalizing Christian spiritual life and Christian congregations. The author reminds us that this is but the beginning of the journey, and "whatever a new kind of Christian is, no one is one yet. . . . But every transformation has to start somewhere." For all who are searching for a deeper life with God and a more honest statement of authentic Christian faith, *A New Kind of Christian* will open the way for an exciting spiritual adventure into new territory and new ways of believing, belonging, and becoming.

Brian D. McLaren is the founding pastor of Cedar Ridge Community Church in the Washington-Baltimore area and the author of four previous books on contemporary Christianity, including *The Church on the Other Side: Doing Ministry in the Postmodern Matrix* (2000) and *The Story We Find Ourselves In: Further Adventures of a New Kind of Christian* (Jossey-Bass, 2003).

The Story We Find Ourselves In: Further Adventures of a New Kind of Christian

BRIAN D. McLAREN

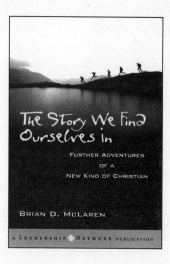

Hardcover / ISBN: 0–7879–6387–9

"A blessing of a book that can alter your view of yourself, your church, and your world."

> —Len Sweet, Stanley E. Jones Chair of Evangelism, Drew University; visiting professor, George Fox University; and chief contributor, Preachingplus.com

"As with A New Kind of Christian, once I started reading this book I could not possibly put it down. Be prepared once again to go on the adventure of having your heart and mind feeling both comforted and uncomfortable, stimulated and stirred, challenged and changed, agreeing and disagreeing, as you join Neo, Dan, and some new faces on their continuing spiritual discovery and journey."

> —Dan Kimball, author, *The Emerging Church: Vintage Christianity for New Generations,* and pastor, Graceland/Santa Cruz Bible Church

"Brian McLaren has given us a wonderful gift a book that helps the calloused, the curious, and the convinced to reimagine the story of God, this marvelous and mysterious story we can all find ourselves in."

> —Dieter Zander, cofounder, ReImagine!, San Francisco

In the spirit of C.S. Lewis' *Screwtape Letters,* McLaren tells an intriguing tale that captures the new spirit of a relevant Christianity, where traditional divisions and doctrinal differences must give way to a focus on God and God's dream for this world. A sequel to *A New Kind of Christian: A Tale of Two Friends on a Spiritual Journey*—new adventures unfold for the old friends and a few new ones.

Brian D. Mclaren is the founding pastor of Cedar Ridge Community Church in the Washington-Baltimore area and the author of four previous books on contemporary Christianity, including *The Church on the Other Side: Doing Ministry in the Postmodern Matrix* (2000) and *A New Kind of Christian: A Tale of Two Friends on a Spiritual Journey* (Jossey-Bass, 2001).

All That's Holy:
A Young Guy, an Old
Car, and the Search
for God in America

Tom Levinson

Hardcover / ISBN: 0–7879–6166–3

"Tom Levinson has written an engaging and lucid personal essay on a timely and timeless subject"

—Joyce Carol Oates

"Tom Levinson has given us a spiritual Odyssey, an extended adventure in the new meaning of faith and hope. Eloquent, heartfelt, and true, this is a book America needs."

—James Carroll, author, *Constantine's Sword: The Church and the Jews* and *American Requiem*, winner of the National Book Award

"This is the best introduction to what is really going on in the multicolored religious lives of our dappled population you can lay hands on today."

—From the Foreword by Harvey Cox, author, *Common Prayers: Faith, Family, and a Christian's Journey Through the Jewish Year*

Meet "Rabbi Least Heat-Moon." It's spiritual pilgrimage, *Blue Highways*-style. From mosque to synagogue to chapel to coffee shop, Tom Levinson's conversations with the faithful and the seeking get to the heart—and relevance—of religion in America today. This conversational collage is set against the backdrop of the author's deepening appreciation—both intellectually and spiritually—of his own Jewish roots.

Tom Levinson is a graduate of Harvard Divinity School, and a former student of Harvey Cox. Formerly the Development Director for the National Interfaith Committee for Worker Justice in Chicago, Levinson has written columns for *Beliefnet*, the popular Internet religion magazine, and is currently attending law school at the University of Chicago.

What Would Buffy Do?
The Vampire Slayer
as Spiritual Guide

JANA REISS

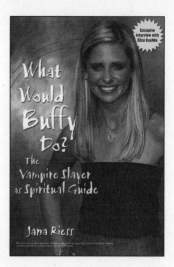

Paper / ISBN: 0–7879–6922–2

"Adds a new dimension to how both fans and critics view the popular series."

—*Publishers Weekly*

"A major contribution to our understanding of Buffy and twenty-first century spirituality. What Would Buffy Do? *may be the best brief introduction to all aspects of this amazing television series."*

—David Lavery, coeditor, *Slayage: The Online International Journal of Buffy Studies*

"Jana Riess brilliantly articulates how the Slayer's battle against evil celebrates the core spiritual values held dear by people of faith. Rock it, Sister Riess!"

—Nancy Holder, author; BTVS: *The Watcher's Guide,* Volume 1; *The Evil That Men Do;* and Immortal

What Would Buffy Do? explores the fascinating spiritual, religious, and mythological ideas of television's hit series *Buffy the Vampire Slayer*—from apocalypse and sacrifice to self-reliance, redemption, and the need for humor when fighting our spiritual battles.

After saving the world as a Brownie, **Jana Riess** went on to earn a master of divinity degree from Princeton Theological Seminary and a Ph.D. in religion from Columbia University. She is the religion book review editor at *Publishers Weekly*. Her favorite character is Giles. Or maybe Spike. Or actually, it's Buffy. Yeah, definitely Buffy.